COMMUNITY POLICING
IN A RURAL SETTING

SECOND EDITION

QUINT C. THURMAN
Southwest Texas State University

EDMUND F. MCGARRELL
Michigan State University

Routledge
Taylor & Francis Group

LONDON AND NEW YORK

Community Policing in a Rural Setting, Second Edition

First published 2003 by Anderson Publishing

Published 2015 by Routledge
2 Park Square, Milton Park, Abingdon, Oxon OX14 4RN

and by Routledge
711 Third Avenue, New York, NY 10017

Routledge is an imprint of the Taylor & Francis Group, an informa business

Library of Congress Cataloging-in-Publication Data

Thurman, Quint C.
   Community policing in a rural setting / Quint C. Thurman, Edmund F. McGarrell.-- 2nd ed.
      p. cm.
   Includes bibliographical references and index.
    ISBN 978-1-58360-534-9 (pbk)
       1. Police, rural--United States. 2. Community policing--United States. I. McGarrell,
   Edmund F., 1956- II. Title.
   HV7965 .T58 2002
   363.2'3'091734--dc21

                                        2001053874

ISBN-13: 978-1-58360-534-9 (pbk)

Cover design by Tin Box Studio, Inc.

EDITOR Elisabeth Roszmann Ebben
ACQUISITIONS EDITOR Michael C. Braswell

Acknowledgments

The authors would like to acknowledge their gratitude to the 18 other contributors to this edition, the numerous practitioners, scholars, and friends who have been instrumental in the development of community policing in classrooms and law enforcement agencies across this country, and the wonderful folks at Anderson, who make publishing an enjoyable process. We would especially like to express our thanks to Biz Ebben for her patience and encouragement during the copyediting process and to Mickey Braswell for his friendship and dependability. Once again, we take responsibility for any defects in this product and count on our readers to set us straight for the next edition.

Contents

Section I
The Challenge of Community Policing in Rural and Small-Town America

Community Policing in a Rural Setting: An Introduction

Quint C. Thurman
Southwest Texas State University

Edmund F. McGarrell
Michigan State University

Introduction

A few years ago, one of the authors attended a curriculum building session on community policing at the Federal Law Enforcement Training Center (FLETC) in Glynco, Georgia. Several practitioners and a few scholars met to develop a train-the-trainer program that FLETC could take on the road to encourage the spread of community policing in rural and small-town America. The first edition of this book was inspired by the group that met and the enthusiasm and wisdom they brought to the session; this second edition is a tribute to the eventual success of the community policing movement across the United States.

While community policing still tends to be many things to many people, the fuzziness of this concept has receded somewhat and the enthusiasm continues. However, having said this, many uncertainties around this issue remain, and agencies wishing to do community policing on purpose will have many questions that make good sense to ask. This new edition addresses many of the challenges we believe that law enforcement agencies in the rural U.S. are facing as we enter the twenty-first century. Readers of the previous edition will find this book to be entirely new in some places; and in places where the articles might seem familiar, most have been updated from the original edition.

Key Issues

The Challenge of Community Policing

Business leaders in the U.S. know that as America changes, so must its organizations. Similarly, leaders in law enforcement agencies must change or risk losing the confidence of taxpayers and, ultimately, "losing market share" to the private security industry. After all, what community wants to pay for additional officers when they believe that the local cops are uninterested in the things that concern them the most regarding their safety?

Law enforcement executives wishing to change from a traditional, professional model of policing must overcome many obstacles. In addition to changing how police personnel carry out their operations in the field, there also are the issues of how to form partnerships with community members and groups and the even greater challenge of organizational change. But change does not come easily.

Realizing the need for help is the first step in effective problem solving. It is also the first step in trying to change an organization or its operations. When community policing first achieved notoriety as a term with which sheriffs and police chiefs were familiar, there was much resistance to the idea that this was anything useful. As time passed, resistance took on new forms. For some executives, community policing could not succeed because "the troops would never buy into it"; for others, it seemed to be a fad that surely would pass if it were ignored. And finally, there was the most subtle resistance of all—giving in to its popularity and claiming to embrace it without ever really digging deep enough to find out what community policing actually means.

Like practitioners, university scholars have been no less guilty in their skepticism. First introduced by A.C. Germann in 1969 and reinforced in an article by John Angell (1971), the concept of community policing was a response to the need to develop a more democratic style of policing that fit a modern society undergirded by a strong constitutional form of government. However, since Herman Goldstein first wrote on the topic of problem-oriented policing in 1979—one of the key components of community policing—academicians have largely failed to demonstrate a consensus about what community policing is or what it might do for the American public that traditional policing had failed to deliver.

Kelling (1988) and Trojanowicz and Bucqueroux (1990) were some of the first scholars to draw much favorable attention to the potential of community policing nearly two decades after the essays by Germann and Angell. About the same time, however, several contributors to Greene and Mastrofski's edited book (1988) raised many issues critical of this new direction for policing. While many of the points that were made were not intentionally meant to derail the progress of community policing, it may have had that effect among practitioners looking for answers. The latter would have to wait a bit for the academic dust to settle if scholarship were to lead practice.

Dennis Rosenbaum's *The Challenge of Community Policing: Testing the Promises* (1994) made a good step in this direction by presenting evaluation data from several community policing experiences, as did several others that followed. But what about community policing in small-town and rural America?

At its most basic level, community policing involves partnerships between citizens and law enforcement agents. Even though one hurdle to community policing remains the development of favorable citizen-police interactions beyond those that the police usually maintain (citizen as complainant, victim, witness, or criminal offender), the other, more challenging obstacle concerns the organization itself (see Zhao and Thurman, 1996, or Thurman et al., 2001).

A central argument throughout this book is that while external, programmatic changes are important in and of themselves, reassessing organizational goals and then reconfiguring an organization so that community policing can be accomplished may be more of an "impossible mandate" than that of policing itself, as Manning (1995) first implied. And yet, as some of the contributions to this book suggest, some organizations are doing just what was thought to be impossible only a few years ago.

The Need for Change

Some of us who are old enough to remember might appreciate the similarities between community policing and the fictional Mayberry police department of television fame. Many Americans, if they are familiar with the television version of rural policing from reruns of the 1950s sitcom the *Andy Griffith Show*, might recall the problem-solving wisdom and good-natured service orientation of the local sheriff, who knew the needs of the good citizens of Mayberry. And, despite the good intentions of his more rule-minded sidekick, Deputy Barney Fife, Sheriff Taylor seemed to know the difference between effectiveness and efficiency. That is, he knew when to take people off the streets for their own good and the good of the townspeople and when to use homespun counseling (and humor) to solve problems.

It seemed to matter less to the fictional Sheriff Taylor that the letter of the law be obeyed for society to function, than that the legal codes were more often a guide for what ought to be done for society to function well; in Mayberry, justice was better achieved through common sense and common decency than common law. However, modern society is far more complex than rural North Carolina of the 1950s. In fictional Mayberry, Sheriff Taylor was the organization and, even though communication could get fouled up and the goals of the organization temporarily abandoned, all could be righted in 30 minutes of airtime. But even Will Rogers, who never met a man he didn't like, would be hard pressed to discern the endearing qualities of a crack dealer, the latter being a character with which the Mayberry of the 1950s was never forced to contend.

Anthony Bouza, a retired Minneapolis police chief and perhaps the most eloquent spokesperson for democratic policing, preaches a view of law enforcement that challenges the professional model of policing often associated with big cities after World War II. In opposition to the reactive style of policing espoused by L.A.P.D. legends William Parker and Daryl Gates, Bouza (1990:227) challenges "war on crime" thinking and the weapons that we might use to fight it by considering the larger issues about the origins of crime itself and how we might work together to solve community problems that fuel crime and disorder.

We recognize that, for some scholars, community policing simply is old wine in new bottles (e.g., Manning, 1988, 1989). That is, it is really no more than basic, professional policing done right. For others, including ourselves, it ranges from an extension of rural or small-town policing that seeks primarily to safeguard public safety and maintain order to a revolutionary concept by which the police are mobilized to tackle a wide range of crime-related and other social problems that affect the quality of daily living.

Discussion

Organization of This Book

In Chapter 2, authors Gary Cordner and Kathryn Scarborough describe what community policing looks like in rural America. While many community policing programs might sound alike and at a glance may appear very similar from one place to the next, variations occur across rural settings. More importantly, for our purposes here, Cordner and Scarborough remind us that vast differences between rural and urban agencies and the citizens each serves often mean big differences in the kinds of approaches that are taken to deliver community policing.

Carl Hawkins, Jr. and Ralph Weisheit in Chapter 3 update our readers with information from recent studies on the nature of crime and policing in rural America. In particular, this chapter examines the extent to which rural law enforcement agencies apply community policing principles to everyday operations and whether these organizations are interested in additional community policing training. Although many agencies have received some introductory community policing training, there remains an unmet need for instruction beyond this level.

In Chapter 4, authors Jihong Zhao and Quint Thurman once again present data from a national subsample of rural police organizations to examine how far community policing has come and what factors they believe have aided or hindered such a transition. Picking up from where Hawkins and Weisheit left off in the previous chapter, the information presented in this chapter focuses on internal organizational change issues and contrasts these with change that occurs outside the organization itself, where change seems to be occurring at a faster pace.

Chapter 5 marks the beginning of a new section of the book that covers internal organizational change issues in rural agencies. Andy Giacomazzi describes how many rural agencies in western American counties have benefited from organizational and community assessments as preliminary steps toward the change to community policing. The author touches on important issues such as identifying organizational values, goals, and structure.

Authors Jim Frank and John Liederbach examine work routines and how police officers ordinarily interact with citizens in small towns and rural areas in Chapter 6. Their observations of 11 jurisdictions from southwestern Ohio lead them to conclude that rural law enforcement agencies already benefit to some extent from close ties between patrol officers and the citizens they serve.

In Chapter 7, noted police scholar John Crank discusses the role of police culture as a forgotten resource that must be included in organizational change efforts. While it is true that human nature in itself tries to resist change and uncertainty, this tendency can be overcome if we understand that change is difficult and realize that agency experience among people in the field is an important asset that must not be overlooked. Crank suggests that mid-level managers and the wisdom that they can bring to bear as problem-solvers should be celebrated as a great resource for agency reform rather than feared or neglected.

In Chapter 8, Ed McGarrell, Rosanne London, and Socorro Benitez discuss the ways in which law enforcement executives can learn more about their employees' values and preferences. Relying on various examples, McGarrell and his coauthors describe the use of formal employee surveys to systematically tap employee opinions. In addition, they introduce focus group interviews as a good method for gaining more in-depth information that can be used for immediate problem-solving.

Chapter 9, written by Ricky Gutierrez and Quint Thurman, centers on issues related to the selection, training, and retention of employees who might be assigned to do community policing work. The authors examine departmental procedures for hiring and evaluating officer performance and suggest how these might be changed to include input from the citizens the agency serves.

Chapter 10 marks the beginning of the third section of the book. Here the discussion of community policing moves from an internal organizational change focus to external organizational change issues. Author David Duffee examines the issue of community and discusses the nature of police-citizen interactions in Chapter 10. In the conclusion of this chapter, the author provides an account of seven typical problems that agencies face in encounters with the public and suggests some issues that agency executives consider in their responses to these problems.

The progression of policing in one rural law enforcement agency is highlighted by Michael Brand and Michael Birzer in Chapter 11. Their work with a small police department in Oklahoma shows how agency adaptation to the need for change can create momentum for change to occur through better training and problem-solving. Using a before-and-after survey approach to measure how the public views police effectiveness over time, the authors observe that public perceptions about crime can be favorably affected by the implementation of community policing in a town of 1,500 residents.

Ed McGarrell, Socorro Benitez, and Ricky Gutierrez suggest useful ways for police agencies to get to know their communities better in Chapter 12. Similar to the methods introduced in Chapter 8 for agency executives to better acquaint themselves with their employees, McGarrell and his coauthors shift their focus to how best to obtain feedback from citizens in general, using pencil-and-paper mail surveys, and how best to collect information from special populations who typically are more difficult to reach with the self-administered questionnaire.

Getting to know a community better is one thing, but actually coming up with workable problem-solving strategies is another as Carl Hawkins, Jr. tells us in Chapter 13. Here we see an actual example of working through a collaborative problem-solving exercise in Hillsborough County, Florida, involving concerted training, education, and apprehension efforts aimed at reducing auto thefts in unincorporated areas of the county.

Chapter 14 illustrates another example of collaborative problem-solving that more directly involves citizens in both the design and development of a problem-solving partnership. Authors Dave Mueller, Quint Thurman, and Cary Heck introduce the "Neutral Zone" as one community policing program that demonstrates that successful police work need not be only reactive. After overcoming substantial political resistance to the idea of providing a safe hangout for gang members, gang wannabes, and other at-risk youths, the Mountlake Terrace Police Department and a broad-based coalition of citizens' groups formed a public-private venture to create an effective problem-solving intervention that not only helped problem teens reintegrate into society, but worked to substantially reduce crime at the same time.

Chapter 15, by Ralph Weisheit and Steven Kernes, concludes the book with a forecast of where rural America is heading in the decades to follow. In particular, the authors examine the impact of three factors that will strongly influence how policing is carried out in rural jurisdictions. Changes in population composition, the economy, and technology offer specific challenges that rural communities will face in the years ahead.

Conclusion

What we hope that this book accomplishes in its 15 chapters is to provide stepping stones for continuing organizational change to community policing. While change is inevitable, making change happen in a particular way is no easy task. And from our experience, sheriffs and chiefs tend to be a bit skeptical—you can't just tell them what you *think* might work, you need to provide good examples of successes already achieved elsewhere.

We hope that the readers of this volume will find the material that we have selected both useful and encouraging. To the extent that they do, we credit the hard work of all 18 contributors. It has been our pleasure to work with each of them, many of them for the second time around.

Now we invite you to read on and discover information that will help you or the agency you might work for in the future shape and fulfill its goals. We hope to fill our next volume with your success stories. After all, your experiences will be the true test of the merits of this book.

References

Angell, J. (1971). "Toward an Alternative to the Classic Police Organizational Arrangement: A Democratic Model." *Criminology* 8:185-206.

Bouza, A. (1990). *The Police Mystique: An Insider's Look at Cops, Crime, and the Criminal Justice System*. New York, NY: Plenum Press.

Germann, A.C. (1969). "Community Policing: An Assessment." *Journal of Criminal Law, Criminology and Police Science* 60:89-96.

Goldstein, H. (1979). "Improving Policing: A Problem-Oriented Approach." *Crime and Delinquency* 25:236-258.

Greene, J., and S. Mastrofski (1988). *Community Policing: Rhetoric or Reality?* New York, NY: Praeger.

Kelling, G.L. (1988). "Police and Communities: The Quiet Revolution." *Perspectives on Policing*, No. 1. Washington, DC: National Institute of Justice and Harvard University.

Manning, P. (1995). "The Police: Mandate, Strategies, and Appearances." In V. Kappeler (ed.), *The Police and Society: Touchstone Readings*. Prospect Heights, IL: Waveland Press, Inc.

_____ (1989). "Community Policing." In R. Dunham and G. Alpert (eds.), *Critical Issues in Policing: Contemporary Readings*. Prospect Heights, IL: Waveland Press, Inc.

_____ (1988). "Community Policing as a Drama of Control." In J. Greene and S. Mastrofski (eds.), *Community Policing: Rhetoric or Reality?* New York, NY: Praeger.

Rosenbaum, D. (1994). *The Challenge of Community Policing: Testing the Promises*. Thousand Oaks, CA: Sage Publications.

Thurman, Q.C., J. Zhao, and A. Giacomazzi (2001). *Community Policing in a Community Era*. Los Angeles, CA: Roxbury.

Trojanowicz, R., and B. Bucqueroux (1990). *Community Policing: A Contemporary Perspective*. Cincinnati, OH: Anderson Publishing Co.

Zhao, J., and Q. Thurman (1996). "The Nature of Community Policing Innovations: Do the Ends Justify the Means?" Washington, DC: Police Executive Research Forum.

Operationalizing Community Policing in Rural America: Sense and Nonsense   2

Gary W. Cordner
Eastern Kentucky University

Kathryn E. Scarborough
Eastern Kentucky University

Introduction

The application of community policing to rural areas and small towns presents some interesting ironies and contradictions. For example:

- Community policing was developed in the 1980s primarily as a big-city strategy for reducing fear of crime and improving police-community relations (Kelling, 1988). As such, it might seem unsuitable for smaller and more rural jurisdictions.

- Some of the specific programs most associated with community policing, such as foot patrol, bicycle patrol, and mini-stations, certainly seem more appropriate for cities than for rural areas.

- To some observers, however, community policing is largely an effort by urban police agencies to decentralize and create "villages within the city" in order to capture the advantages that naturally accrue to smaller-scale departments. In this sense, urban police seem to see community policing as a way to become more like small-town police.

- Also, many small-town and rural police steadfastly insist that community policing is what they have always done. They often point out that they actually know most of the people whom they police, and that they handle many matters informally by using their discretion.

- Ironically, however, while urban police seek to emulate their country cousins, and while rural police often come by community policing naturally, many rural and small-town police officers yearn to do "real police work." By this they mean more action, more arrests, and even a more formal and aloof stance toward the public. It seems as if Joe Friday of *Dragnet* and Andy Taylor of *Mayberry RFD* each think the other has it better.

In this chapter we hope to clarify such contradictions. The next section identifies three key varieties of small-town/rural policing and four important dimensions of community policing. The rest of the chapter discusses how these dimensions of community policing apply to different types of small-town and rural jurisdictions. Throughout the chapter we seek to distinguish between commonsense applications of community policing and illogical distortions.

Key Issues

There is a lot of variety to rural America—vast farming areas in the Midwest, huge ranches in the southwest, the Rocky Mountains, the Appalachian mountain region, the Mississippi delta, small towns of many different shapes, and so forth. Some rural areas are fairly close to cities, whereas others are very remote. Some are relatively affluent, others quite poor. It is important to keep this rural variation in mind whenever considering policing issues (see also Weisheit, Falcone & Wells, 1999).

It is helpful to think in terms of three basic structural varieties of rural policing:

- **Small-Town Police.** These are small municipal police departments, normally headed by appointed chiefs. One should recognize, however, that not all small police departments are rural—many are located within metropolitan areas.

- **Rural Sheriffs.** These are county-wide agencies, normally headed by elected sheriffs. Some sheriff's departments cover jurisdictions that include both rural and nonrural areas, some are totally rural, and a few have primarily urban jurisdictions. It should be noted that many sheriff's departments, including some with largely rural areas, are fairly large organizations, due to their county-wide responsibilities.

- **Rural State Police.** These are statewide agencies, usually headed by appointed commissioners. Some state police agencies operate exclusively as highway patrols, while others have generalist police duties. In either case, state police agencies are all large organizations and they typically deploy most of their officers to rural regions, because there is less demand for their services in metropolitan and urban areas.

When thinking about rural policing in America, including rural community policing, it is essential to include small-town police, rural sheriffs, and rural state police in the picture. Nationally, each plays an important role. To complicate things, though, these roles vary from one state to the next (Reaves & Goldberg, 1998).

Sheriff's departments dominate rural policing in some states and are nearly irrelevant in others. Much the same can be said for state police. Also, some states have many small-town police departments (per capita), whereas in other states the police system is more consolidated and comprised of fewer, larger departments.

To organize our thinking about how community policing might apply to these different rural policing scenarios, it will help to consider four dimensions of community policing (Cordner, 2000):

- **The Philosophical Dimension.** This includes the ideas, beliefs, attitudes, and values that underlie community policing, such as community input, broad function of police work, and personal service.

- **The Strategic Dimension.** This includes the key operational concepts that translate community policing philosophy into policies, priorities, and reallocation of resources, such as reoriented operations, geographic focus, and prevention emphasis.

- **The Tactical Dimension.** This includes the concrete programs, tactics, and behaviors that officers implement when they actually perform community policing, such as positive interaction, partnerships, and problem solving.

- **The Organizational Dimension.** This includes changes in police organizational structure, management, and information systems that may need to be made in order to support and facilitate the implementation of community policing.

In the following section we discuss the practical application of each of these dimensions of community policing within the different contexts of rural policing.

Discussion

Small-Town Police

A component of the philosophical dimension that especially affects small-town policing is the broad function of police work. Small-town police inevitably perform a variety of tasks, many unrelated to modern stereotypical views of policing. Small-town policing is not often dominated by law enforcement activities, which constitute the "real police work" mentioned earlier. Instead, small-town policing may naturally be more service-oriented, with fewer law enforcement and order-maintenance activities. Interestingly, however, in an effort to emphasize more legalistic activities, small-town police may seek to narrow their focus to "real police work," even though these opportunities are relatively minimal (Kraska & Cubellis,

1997). This sometimes results in rather oppressive levels of enforcement of minor traffic and minor public order offenses.

Citizen input can be both more and less accessible, depending on the town. Because officers will likely get to know citizens in their respective communities, it might be expected that citizen input would be more readily available. At the level of the individual officer, this may be the case, but at the organizational level, where citizen input to larger departments is often solicited via mail surveys, meetings, or telephone calls, citizen input in small-town policing may be more limited. The availability of fewer organizational resources can interfere with the use of such techniques, as can the small town's receptivity to such formal devices; sometimes, the chief's or town leaders' real desire for widespread citizen input on policies, priorities, or other issues is also debatable.

One specific challenge for small-town police, in regard to the strategic dimension of community policing, relates to reoriented operations. Because small towns are small, patrol officers can actually hope to cover their beats (often the entire town) thoroughly, several times a shift. Because they can create a substantial level of visibility (an objective that many big-city, county-level, and state police recognize as unattainable), they may be reluctant to divert patrol time to other types of activities. Also, because the call-for-service workload is not that heavy in many small towns, there is less of a sense of urgency about the need to find different ways of conducting police operations. Thus, the acceptability of such modern alternatives as telephone reporting, directed patrol, foot patrol, or case screening in a small town is more problematic and depends more on proven necessity than just on the fact that "everybody else is doing it." This higher burden of proof may make it tough for small-town chiefs to justify and sell such innovations to their officers and to the community. On the plus side, though, it also puts a brake on the common tendency to just adopt the latest police fad, without regard to its suitability to local needs and conditions.

The tactical element of partnerships may need to take different forms in small towns as opposed to urban areas. Such devices as citizen patrols, "take back the streets" campaigns, major clean-ups, and even neighborhood watch may not make sense in many small towns as techniques for getting citizens more involved in protecting their communities. What may make more sense are police-community partnerships to provide activities for youth ("there's nothing to do around here"), partnerships to serve senior citizens, partnerships to address domestic violence and child abuse, citizen volunteers who perform clerical duties for the police department, and similar programs. The key is to design partnerships and forms of citizen involvement that address real small-town issues without seeming either phony or overly formal.

Small-town problem solving may have several distinctive features. For one, problem identification (scanning) should occur effortlessly and efficiently—it would be quite surprising to have an unrecognized hot spot in a small town. It might also be the case, however, that recordkeeping is less systematic and thorough in many small towns, so that scanning and analysis depend more on personal observation and human memory, each of which is notoriously faulty. Also related to analysis, the unfortunate tendency of officers to assume that they already know everything about a problem, including what causes it, may be even greater in small towns because they know the people involved and much of the history and context of the problem. This kind of intimate knowledge generally helps in problem solving, of course, but can interfere if it precludes objective analysis. Yet another impediment to small-town problem solving can arise at the response stage—generally, officers probably have access to fewer types of referral services and collaboration opportunities in small towns. Officers may have to be more creative and resourceful themselves, because there are fewer other service providers than would be found in a metropolitan area to help out with problem solving.

In small-town police organizations, decentralization may not be a necessary prerequisite to community policing because existing structures are not as centralized or hierarchical as those more commonly seen in larger municipal departments. This is affected by the small number of officers in the organization, which often results in an already flattened structure with one person "in charge" and everybody else at the second level. With only one person or a limited number of people in supervisory positions, however, management styles may warrant change. Instead of the more traditional authoritative, disciplinary model of management, a style that emphasizes employee empowerment, rewards, and input would be more amenable to the community policing philosophy in a small-town police agency. This would also seem warranted because actual supervision is slight in most small-town departments, and because lowly patrol officers are often the highest ranking officials on duty.

Because applicant pools for small-town police organizations tend to be smaller and more homogeneous than in other types of police organizations, personnel diversity can be especially troublesome. Not only do organizations have limited female and minority applicants, these employees are often difficult to retain. Characteristically, women and minorities have found it difficult to compete and remain in larger municipal agencies; some research suggests that there may be additional unique stressors for them in smaller, more rural departments (Bartol, Bergen, Volckens & Knoras, 1992), making recruitment and retention even more difficult. Hence, the goal of a diverse police organization may be especially difficult to achieve in smaller towns.

Rural Sheriffs

Because sheriffs are elected officials and their employees often serve at the pleasure of the sheriff (without any civil service protection), beliefs and attitudes of the officers (or deputies) may be more directly affected by their bosses' stated interests than in other types of police organizations. This can have a significant effect on the entire organizational culture, both positively and negatively. It probably means that a sheriff who is firmly committed to community policing has some advantages, compared to an appointed chief, in convincing his or her employees to adopt similar beliefs and implement community policing.

The broad function of community policing may be more readily seen in sheriff's departments because of the tendency to operate with a less legalistic approach, due to political effects on the organization as well as historical differences in the role of the sheriff (Falcone & Wells, 1995). There may be a focus on more service-related activities or those that are seen as less politically damaging than, perhaps, writing speeding tickets, to please the sheriff's constituents. Additionally, citizen input may be at least minimally solicited, because a sheriff who loses touch with the voters is likely to end up unemployed.

The strategic element of geographic focus has a natural appeal for sheriff's departments, in order to give each county resident "their own deputy" and also to improve each deputy's local knowledge, which is crucial for efficient service of criminal and civil papers (warrants, subpoenas, etc.). Reoriented operations may provide a challenge, however. Because the sheriff is an elected official, sheriff's departments tend to emphasize personal service to their clientele (voters). If workload increases to the point that difficult choices have to be made about cutting patrol coverage or slowing response times to nonemergency calls, the risk of alienating voters sometimes directly interferes with modern police strategy. Some sheriffs may end up continuing what they know to be largely ineffective strategies because they fear rejection at the ballot box.

Partnerships and collaboration in the rural county setting may have some features distinctive from either small towns or big cities. Key players are likely to be such groups as farm and electric co-ops, farm bureaus, 4-H and FFA clubs, and agricultural extension services. The mere fact of distance plays a role—distance between peoples' homes, distance to town, distance to the offices of service providers, etc. Also, while a long-standing sense of community may aid the development of partnerships in rural counties, the parallel senses of rugged individualism and privacy that characterize many rural areas may impede collective action. Finally, the fact that the sheriff is an elected official from one political party may reduce the enthusiasm of members of other parties for joining in partnerships with deputies.

Because sheriff's departments, even rural ones, vary widely in size, the applicability of decentralizing or flattening as an organizational approach to community policing is situational. Attempts at flattening or decentralizing may be made easier due to the unrestricted authority of the sheriff over the organization, but they may also be more difficult because of the political nature of the organization and the effects of restructuring on the job security of the sheriff's political supporters. Personnel diversity in sheriff's departments is generally greater than in small-town departments or state police organizations, but nevertheless is often lacking with regard to both women and minorities. The problem of attracting and retaining women and minorities persists throughout the law enforcement community, and sheriff's departments are no exception.

Rural State Police

The population of state police organizations is less consistent with regard to "community policing" authority than are small-town police agencies and sheriff's departments—some state police agencies have limited authority only on interstate and state highways, while others have complete authority throughout the state. Highway patrols, particularly, could have a problem adopting the broad view of the police function associated with community policing. For them, a more narrow function with regard to police work is by law, rather than simply departmental philosophy (although even they could take a broad approach to their highway safety mandate). Full-service state police agencies are not as narrowly constrained by law, but their image also tends to emphasize law enforcement and traffic enforcement to the exclusion of other types of duties (Falcone, 1998).

State police agencies do not seem to actively solicit citizen input regarding the performance of their duties, especially at the organizational level. Perhaps at the individual trooper level there is more probability that citizen input may be sought or accepted, but by and large the state police as an organization seem to function rather autonomously without input from anyone but their political superiors in state government. Such input is perhaps not terribly necessary as long as the agency's mission is simply to enforce traffic and criminal laws throughout the state, but if the state police function is broader, including problem solving, making communities safer, and so forth, then local input becomes crucial.

Geographic focus and accountability would seem to be concepts that should be important for state police organizations, in order to accomplish the daunting task of providing services and controlling employees over entire states. State police typically employ posts, detachments, or other geographic subunits, and some officially deploy so-called resident troopers. Accountability is often complicated, however, where state police share jurisdiction over geographic areas with other agencies, especially sheriff's departments. Further, many state police agencies have fallen prey to two tendencies over the past decade or two that interfere with geographic focus: (1) creeping specialization, which leaves fewer troopers for generalist police duties; and (2) an ever-increasing emphasis on highway safety, which tends to direct attention away from communities and toward interstate and state highways. Consequently, the once-typical mode of state policing, in which a trooper served as the primary police service provider in a county or portion of a county, was well known, and possibly even lived in the community, seems far less common today.

The state police are agencies that ought to embrace prevention, given our experiences in the traffic safety arena, in which engineering and education have long been recognized as being at least as effective as enforcement in reducing accidents and fatalities. By their nature, however, many state police agencies seem to take a particularly legalistic, enforcement-oriented approach to dealing with all types of problems, including crime, disorder, and traffic. Looked at another way, state police agencies may be the most proactive of all types of police organizations, due to their traffic control responsibilities, but their proactivity seems to be focused almost entirely on enforcement, rather than on any other approaches to prevention or problem solving.

The tactical element of positive interaction may be one that many state police agencies have overlooked or forgotten as an easy method for implementing community policing. Inevitably, much of the official interaction that troopers have with the public occurs in the traffic enforcement context, and while such interactions need not always be negative, they are rarely completely positive from the perspective of the citizen. To balance these types of interactions, rural troopers might want to regularly stop by country stores, farm co-ops, gas stations, and similar establishments for a friendly visit and to pick up the latest local news. Also, a few conversations across a country fence can go a long way toward showing one's interest and concern and laying the groundwork for later problem solving or cooperation with investigations.

Because state police organizations are usually larger than small-town police or sheriff's departments, decentralization and flattening of the hierarchy may be more appropriate and more important as facilitators of community policing. Flattening of the structure may be appropriate at the post level too, because these tend to be mini-organizations in and of themselves.

Most current management and leadership styles in state police organizations do not support community policing. Styles that advocate less autocratic control and increased employee empowerment would be more effective, but are quite unlike those found in most state police organizations. An emphasis on a less legalistic, more service-based approach would also embrace community policing more than the approach currently used by most state police organizations.

Diversity in state police organizations is extremely limited. Of the three types of rural policing organizations discussed, the state police have the most homogeneous organization, consisting mostly of white males. Special efforts must be made to diversify state police organizations, which epitomize law enforcement as a closed occupation reserved only for those who fit the traditional image of those who do "real police work," thereby excluding women and minorities.

Conclusion

Community policing is every bit as applicable to small towns and rural areas as it is to big cities and suburbs, but how it can be implemented, which techniques make sense, and what aspects of community policing are most problematic vary, both between rural and urban areas and also across different types of rural situations. Small-town police departments are inherently small; additionally, their officers are often regarded by their constituents, rightly or wrongly, as amateurs. Consequently, small-town police frequently seem to be pursuing professionalization as a means of being taken seriously, sometimes at the expense of the community-oriented characteristics that come more naturally in small towns.

Rural sheriff's departments may be large or small organizations, so the importance of restructuring and revising management styles depends on each agency's particular circumstances. One thing that almost all such organizations have in common, though, is that they are headed by an elected sheriff. This seems to have several implications for community policing—sheriffs tend to favor service orientation and to encourage citizen (voter) input, for example, and they may be able to demand more loyalty and commitment toward implementing community policing from their deputies, many of whom are political appointees lacking civil service protection or much other job security. On the other hand, the requirement for periodic reelection may rob some sheriffs of the opportunity to develop and implement long-term organizational change—even those who win reelection may have to invest much of their attention and energy toward their political well-being. Also, many of their employees may give only partial commitment to the sheriff's organizational strategy, hedging their bets in case the next election brings a new sheriff.

State police agencies are all large organizations—implementing community policing in them involves both large-scale organizational change and also an attack on traditional state police values and cultures, which seem to support more aloof and legalistic styles of policing. Thus, community policing for state police may represent the biggest challenge among the various rural scenarios. It also represents a huge opportunity because the state police provide such a significant portion of rural policing. The reminiscences of older troopers suggest that state policing was once more community-based, at least in some states, and there are numerous efforts under way around the country now to implement community policing within state police agencies. One might argue that if state police can do community policing, any agency can.

References

Bartol, C., G. Bergen, J. Volckens, and K. Knoras (1992). "Women in Small-Town Policing: Job Performance and Stress." *Criminal Justice and Behavior* 19:240-259.

Cordner, G. (2000). "Community Policing: Elements and Effects." In G. Alpert and A. Piquero (ed.), *Community Policing: Contemporary Readings*, Second Edition. Prospect Heights, IL: Waveland Press, Inc.

Falcone, D. (1998). "The Illinois State Police as an Archetypal Model." *Police Quarterly* 1:61-83.

Falcone, D., and L. Wells (1995). "The County Sheriff as a Distinctive Policing Modality." *American Journal of Police* 14:123-149.

Kelling, G. (1988). "Police and Communities: The Quiet Revolution." *Perspectives on Policing*, No. 1. Washington, DC: National Institute of Justice.

Kelling, G., and M. Moore (1988). "The Evolving Strategy of Policing." *Perspectives on Policing*, No. 4. Washington, DC: National Institute of Justice.

Kraska, P., and L. Cubellis (1997). "Militarizing Mayberry and Beyond: Making Sense of American Paramilitary Policing." *Justice Quarterly* 14:607-629.

Reaves, B., and A. Goldberg (1998). "Census of State and Local Law Enforcement Agencies, 1996." *Bulletin*. Washington, DC: Bureau of Justice Statistics.

Weisheit, R., D. Falcone, and L. Wells (1999). *Crime and Policing in Rural and Small-Town America*, Second Edition. Prospect Heights, IL: Waveland Press, Inc.

The State of Community Policing in Small Towns and Rural Areas   3

Carl W. Hawkins, Jr.
Hillsborough County Sheriff's Office

Ralph A. Weisheit
Illinois State University

Introduction

Much has been made of the push toward community policing in America. In 1994, Congress authorized federal expenditures specifically to put more police on the street who would be actively engaged in community policing. Although the 1994 Crime Bill required that one-half of the money distributed for community policing go to rural and small-town departments, little was known about where rural departments were with regard to community policing. It has been suggested that rural and small-town police "have always done community policing," and there is some support for this. It is less clear, however, whether rural departments are systematically engaged in community policing, whether their strategies might be enhanced through training, and whether rural departments would have an interest in receiving training in community policing. This chapter offers a preliminary look at the extent to which rural police are engaged in formal strategies of community policing, and whether they are interested in receiving training in community policing.

The findings reported here are the result of two surveys using the same database. In the first survey, a systematic sample was drawn of counties in the United States with fewer than 50,000 people. These nonmetropolitan counties constitute more than 70 percent of the counties in the United States. One-half of these counties were systematically selected for the study. For each of these counties, a survey was sent to the sheriff and the chief of the largest municipal department in the county (although 20 percent of the counties had no municipal department). This survey concerned general crime problems, training needs, and obstacles to receiving training. A total of 2,022 surveys were mailed (1,124 sheriffs and 898 chiefs), and six weeks later a second survey was sent to nonrespondents. In all, 1,152 surveys (57 percent) were returned. The average department size in the study was 10 full-time officers, with 80 percent of the sample having 20 or fewer officers.

Six months after the initial survey was sent, a second survey was sent to a systematic sample of 400 sheriffs and chiefs who responded to the first survey (195

Less than one-half of the agencies report that they have a:

- Training program for officers in community policing (44%)

- Problem-solving process with a method of analysis (41%)

- Standard operating procedure for community policing (39%)

- Training program for supervisors and managers in community policing (36%)

- Method for handling nonpriority calls for service, such as call screening (34%)

- Performance evaluation that supports community policing (33%)

- Reward system (promotion, assignment, etc.) that promotes community policing (16%)

Interestingly, the internal organizational features most likely to encourage officer involvement in community policing (performance evaluations and reward systems) were among the features least likely to be used by these agencies.

The external organizational features are the programs and practices directly visible to the community. These external organizational features include the following items.

More than one-half of the agencies report that they have:

- Crime prevention programs offered in the school and community (86%)

- Officers involved as members of community organizations (86%)

- Volunteers in their agency (65%)

- Officers assigned to elementary and secondary schools (63%)

- Officers on foot patrol (51%)

Less than one-half of the agencies report that they have:

- A police and community group that meets regularly (38%)

- Officers on bicycles (30%)

- A substation in their agency (26%)

Training. Results of the second survey also reflected a high interest in training. Nearly everyone (96%) indicated that they or someone from their agency would attend a community policing training program specifically designed for small-town and rural law enforcement agencies if the training were free. Most (84%) would attend if a reasonable fee was charged, and for most of these agencies reasonable meant less than $100. Nearly one-half said that they had a facility within 30 miles where training could be conducted.

Just under one-half (40%) reported having had formal training in community policing. These respondents were then asked a series of more specific questions about the training. Of those who said they had received formal training in community policing, the areas in which they were most often trained were the following:

More than one-half of the agencies say that they have received training in:

- Introduction to community policing (91%)

- Techniques and strategies in community engagement and partnership (76%)

- Techniques and strategies in problem solving (68%)

- Strategic planning for community policing (59%)

- Management and supervisor responsibilities in community policing (59%)

- Developing a community policing training course for officers (58%)

- Developing a community policing training course for supervisors and managers (54%)

Less than one-half of the agencies say that they have received training in:

- In-call diversion and/or prioritization (45%)

- Deployment and scheduling of community policing officers (45%)

- Analysis and review of existing models of community policing (44%)

- Crime prevention through environmental design (44%)

- Techniques and strategies for evaluating community policing (41%)

- Performance evaluation for community policing (35%)

- Techniques and strategies in change management (35%)

- Forming and sustaining a community council (34%)

- Developing a prototype for community policing (32%)

- Workload control and information systems (30%)

- Techniques and strategies in survey construction (30%)

- Reward systems to sustain community policing (26%)

In the first survey, chiefs and sheriffs indicated that it was a problem that training was not specifically designed to take the rural and small-town setting into account. It was not surprising then, that of those who received formal training in community policing, only about one-fourth (26%) said the training was specifically designed for small-town and rural law enforcement agencies. Thus, an important training need of these agencies was not being met.

Finally, nearly one-third of the respondents said they knew someone who could assist in designing and developing a community policing training program for small-town and rural police. This suggests that there may be a substantial pool of experts who can be used to create training programs for community policing in small towns and rural areas.

Discussion

The first survey indicated that many of the most serious crime problems facing rural and small-town police are those facing urban police, such as drugs, juvenile crime, and spouse abuse. While rural police indicate an interest in training, they face several obstacles to training, including cost, time, distance, and the fact that many training programs designed for urban police do not take into account the circumstances under which rural and small-town police operate.

The second survey focused more directly on the issue of community policing in rural and small-town departments. Several conclusions can be drawn from this survey. The first concerns the extent to which organizational features of these departments support community policing. About one-half of the agencies studied had a program in community policing, but relatively few had internal or external organizational features that would provide support for community policing activities.

In terms of internal organizational features, few departments had a reward system that promoted community policing and only about one-third used performance evaluations that supported community policing. The internal organizational feature that was present in most of these departments was receiving input from local citizens in determining community problems. Most input appeared to be a feature of daily nonstructured interactions with the community.

Regarding external organizational features, most agencies offered in-school prevention programs, had officers who were involved in community organizations, used volunteers, assigned officers to schools, and had officers on foot patrol. These agencies generally did not have a substation, officers on bicycles, or a police-community group that met regularly.

From these surveys and other research it appears that police-citizen interactions are less formal and structured in rural areas. The interaction between police and the community appears to be less constrained and more natural. This may be more the result of the community and its impact on the police, rather than the reverse. Small towns and rural areas are characterized as homogeneous, with low levels of cultural diversity, less frequent crime, and physical isolation. Officers and citizens have more opportunities to know each other personally in a variety of roles, and this may shape the way they interact when "official" problems arise.

These external and internal features suggest that rural and small-town agencies take a less formal and less structured approach to community policing than is normally seen in more urban areas. The question is whether this less structured approach can be sustained, particularly in communities undergoing change. Further, there are still many unanswered questions about efficiency, effectiveness, and equity in these agencies, compared to their urban counterparts.

Conclusion

One conclusion of this research concerns the need for formal training in community policing in small-town and rural agencies. Most of the agencies in this study report having no formal training in community policing, and when training was reported, there were often substantial blocks of instruction missing. Nearly all who had received training had been exposed to "introduction to community policing." Beyond that, training in special areas was far less frequent. In fact, for 12 of the 19 training areas listed, fewer than one-half of the departments reported having received that block of training.

A final conclusion of this research is that a training program in community policing specifically designed for small-town and rural areas would be supported by these agencies. Nearly every respondent expressed an interest in such training, particularly if the financial costs were minimal.

Overall, there is a strong interest and a strong need for training in community policing among rural and small-town police. This training must take into account the many features of the rural area that makes policing there different from policing in large cities or suburbs. These differences include small department sizes with limited backup, small budgets, and a relative lack of other resources in the community. At the same time, it is clear that rural and small-town departments are ideal targets for such training. Many elements of community policing are already in place as a natural product of the rural environment. These departments are therefore "primed" for training in community policing.

Facilitators and Obstacles to Community Policing in Rural America

4

Jihong Zhao
University of Nebraska at Omaha

Quint C. Thurman
Southwest Texas State University

Introduction

There is a growing body of information about community policing in the United States. In particular, studies about the implementation of community policing and its effectiveness in reducing crime and disorder have appeared with some regularity in the past few years. However, the success of community policing and the lessons learned from it mostly tell about community policing in larger cities. What has been overlooked in most research to date is the implementation of community policing in rural and small-town police agencies.

The purpose of this chapter is to discuss the popularity of community policing in rural law enforcement agencies and the issues that favorably or unfavorably affect its implementation. Relying on data from a national survey of police chiefs from cities with a population less than 40,000 people, we look at three main issues that are linked to the success or failure of community policing. First, we look at the importance that rural police administrators attach to community policing. Second, we examine the popularity of a wide variety of community policing programs among smaller police agencies. Third, we identify facilitators and obstacles to the implementation of community policing in a rural setting.

Key Issues

The importance that police administrators attach to community policing has become increasingly evident in recent years. In order to learn about the level of commitment to community policing in rural America, we looked at recent data from a national survey of 281 police chiefs from 47 states that were collected by the Division of Governmental Studies and Services at Washington State University in 1996. Eighty-four percent of the police chiefs from cities initially included in a representative national sample selected by the International City Management Association in 1969 returned a completed questionnaire. Of those who responded,

34 were employed in police departments located in cities with fewer than 40,000 residents (city size was determined according to 1990 census data).

To examine police chiefs' interests in community policing, three questions were asked. When asked about the importance of community policing to their agencies, 75.9 percent said they believed that community policing programs are highly valuable or somewhat valuable and none reported that they saw no value in them. Furthermore, the large majority (82.8%) reported that their own community policing programs had grown in scale over time.

It also is important to know what kinds of community policing programs in particular are being widely used across the United States in rural jurisdictions. In general, there are two main kinds of community policing programs we recognize, based upon who most directly benefits from them. Some community policing programs largely benefit the organization itself in terms of improving morale and promoting productivity, while other community policing programs are aimed at daily operations and crime prevention activities that provide direct public safety benefits to citizens.

When we asked rural law enforcement executives about the kinds of programs they have implemented in terms of specific changes they have made to their organizations to better accommodate community policing, we found that:

- 75 percent now authorize the first officer at a crime scene to oversee control of the crime scene.

- 62 percent have recently reassessed ranks and assignments in accordance with agency objectives.

- 41 percent have increased the number of civilians they have hired into their organization.

- 41 percent have begun using quality circles (small group problem-solving units).

- 10 percent have made reassignments of some management personnel from sworn personnel to civilian personnel.

- 3 percent have created "master police officer" positions to increase rewards for line officers.

When asked about any external changes they have made that might directly benefit the public and were specifically related to police operations, we found that:

- 100 percent had implemented public educational programs.

- 86 percent had added either a bicycle, foot, or horse patrol to their ordinary patrol schedule.

- 72 percent had created special task forces for problem solving.

- 83 percent had assigned specific officers to a school or neighborhood.

- 62 percent used citizen surveys to help keep informed about local problems.

- 31 percent sponsored a community newsletter.

- 34 percent had a victim contact program.

- 31 percent used police storefronts.

Similarly, when asked about specific crime prevention activities they engaged in to help them in the implementation of community policing, we learned that:

- 90 percent had block watch programs in place.

- 72 percent sent departmental representatives to block watch meetings.

- 62 percent used unpaid civilian volunteers to perform support and community liaison activities.

- 45 percent had business block watch programs.

Specific questions concerning the types of training interests that police administrators thought benefited them the most in implementing community policing also were included in the survey. Statistical analysis helped identify three themes in police chiefs' responses to questions about how best to encourage community policing. Responses here can be grouped into these areas: police-community relations, the role of middle managers in an agency, and performance skills in general.

Average ratings for these three groups of items indicate that police chiefs were most interested in police-community relations and how best to achieve citizen satisfaction concerning their department's efforts. In particular, police chiefs were most interested in police officer ethics and the values that the department conveyed to the public. Only slightly less important were emphases on cultural awareness and minority relations.

Police chiefs also were highly interested in middle manager skills. In particular, they viewed mid-level managers' support for community policing as the most important link to successful implementation, followed by how well middle managers delegated authority and how well middle managers were trained in community policing survival strategies. Slightly less important was mid-level management's knowledge concerning the principles of neighborhood organization.

Finally, police administrators also were found to be interested in general performance skill issues. They were found to be most interested in achieving excellence through the provision of community services, positive risk-taking, and liability awareness. Of lesser importance were understanding and applying quality circles.

Statistical analysis also was used to determine groupings of the obstacles to community policing. Like facilitators, three unique categories were identified by police administrators. The category of obstacles that received the highest average rating involved the problem of doing community policing while simultaneously maintaining emergency response time. This is an item category that reflects a key concern of police chiefs—how can a local police department provide additional community policing services and still keep up with calls for service from their community? It seems likely that police departments who suffer greatly from this obstacle will find it difficult to make a substantial change to community policing, at least initially.

A second category of obstacles concerned internal resistance to change. Departmental confusion concerning what community policing is was the biggest concern in this category, followed closely by the view that community policing training was not readily available and that officers still believed that community policing might be "soft" on crime. Line officer resistance and resistance from mid-level management were the next greatest obstacles, followed by resistance from police unions.

Interestingly, impediments coming from the local community were perceived to be less of a hindrance to community policing than the other two categories of obstacles mentioned above. The difficulty of demonstrating the effectiveness of community policing to the public with regard to reducing crime was seen as the biggest obstacle, followed by the community's concern that community policing is "soft" on crime, civil service rules, and general community resistance. With the exception of the first item, all of these impediments identified by police chiefs were seen only as "slight obstacles" at worst.

Discussion

Programs aimed at changing law enforcement agencies from the inside are developed less frequently than community policing programs that are implemented for the direct benefit of the public. While the data we introduced here suggest that many programs involving the reorientation of police operations and crime prevention are highly popular in agencies located in jurisdictions with less than 40,000 residents, only three internally oriented community policing programs were found to be actively used by more than one-half of the police executives we surveyed. These three involved the authorization of crime scene control, the reassessment of ranks and assignments, and increased civilian hiring.

The popular emphasis on doing community policing to directly benefit citizens is something that also occurs in larger departments throughout the more urban areas of the country. From our experience, we note that most police administrators see their primary mission as involving crime control and not much else. As law enforcement executives begin to realize the benefits of community policing to their organizations, we expect that they will also be encouraged to try other innovations, such as those that might provide direct internal benefits. An effective strategy is for agencies to implement changes in their external work environment first and use those experiences to promote additional risk-taking. Change in one dimension seems to go hand-in-hand with eventual change in the other.

A preference for externally focused community policing programs over internally focused programs also seems evident in terms of the other data we presented. Responses from police chiefs concerning the facilitators and obstacles to community policing implementation suggest that police administrators see greater potential working with the public and perhaps more uncertainty about changing their own organizations.

For example, police chiefs in the sample identified police-community relations as their highest interest area and rated this same area as the one that they believed posed the fewest significant obstacles to community policing implementation. From our experience, we have noted a similar pattern in research on citizen support for community policing. Research by Thurman and Reisig (1996) suggests that residents of rural communities typically are ready to participate in police-community partnerships and simply are waiting for police departments to show them how to proceed.

Where police chiefs in this study saw the greatest need for help was in the actual implementation of community policing. One key obstacle was balancing how to add community policing programs without sacrificing response time. Ironically, this issue continues to trouble both law enforcement executives and those of us who study policing. What the latter have theorized (and there have been some unpublished findings in support of this idea—see McGarrell and Thurman, 1996) is that as public confidence in the police rises, so do the calls for service. At least initially, we warn that police agencies doing community policing well will suffer from higher public expectations. It will not be until some point later that actual crime rates will be reduced as the public gets on board with crime prevention and begins helping police agencies to deter would-be criminals and catch actual criminals before they can do too much harm. However, the advantage of community policing in the long run is communities made safer by the police and citizens working together to look out for common interests.

A final point of discussion concerns organizational obstacles. Some of the key obstacles to change from a traditional law enforcement agency to a community-oriented agency include not knowing what community policing is, worries about it being "soft" on crime, lack of training, and organizational resistance to change. On the other hand, police chiefs acknowledge that support through the training of mid-level managers is of great benefit for successful community policing implementation. Leadership at this level, coming from people trained in community policing principles, is crucial. Supervisors who can inspire innovative community policing activities and are willing to learn new ways to measure line officer performance can make great contributions to organizational change.

Conclusion

The purpose of this chapter was to examine the popularity of community policing in rural law enforcement agencies across the United States. We looked at a number of issues, ranging from community policing values to facilitators and obstacles to community policing implementation. We think a few key points should be emphasized.

First, we continue to find widespread support for the idea of community policing. Second, many of the community policing programs popular in urban areas were also popular in smaller, more rural police departments. Third, most of the more popular programs we noted were aimed at establishing a link between the police and local communities to improve crime control and prevention activities. Agencies seem to support relatively few programs targeted at changing organizations internally for the primary benefit of employees. This continues to be true for large, urban agencies as well (see Thurman, Zhao & Giacomazzi, 2001).

Community policing offers law enforcement executives a great opportunity to deliver public services in a form that citizens say they want. While there undoubtedly are many challenges that police chiefs and sheriffs will have to face if they are going to move their agencies forward, as this chapter has suggested, the more success they experience from joint police-community partnerships, the more they might be encouraged to try to change their agencies organizationally, and in so doing, enjoy deeper and longer-lasting benefits for their employees.

References

McGarrell, E.F., and Q.C. Thurman (1996). *Findings from the 1995 Spokane Police Department Citizen Survey: Final Report*. Spokane, WA: Washington State Institute for Community Oriented Policing.

Thurman, Q.C., and M.D. Reisig (1996). "Community Oriented Research in an Era of Community Oriented Policing." *American Behavioral Scientist* 39:570-586.

Thurman, Q.C., J. Zhao, and A. Giacomazzi (2001). *Community Policing in a Community Era*. Los Angeles, CA: Roxbury.

Section II
Organizational Change
and Community Policing

Assessing the Need for Organizational Change in Rural American Police Agencies 5

Andrew L. Giacomazzi
Boise State University

Introduction

By the end of the twentieth century, neighborhood residents across the United States were joining forces with the police in collaborative partnerships to solve problems related to crime, disorder, and fear. Communities were seeing improvements in the quality of neighborhood life and in satisfaction toward the police in cities, towns, and counties that had implemented a community-based model of policing. For example, success stories had occurred in some of America's largest cities (Chicago Community Policing Evaluation Consortium, 1997), medium-sized cities (Reisig & Parks, 2000) and in rural America (Giacomazzi, Helms & Brody, 2000).

While the community policing literature teems with outcome-based studies concerning the effects of community policing, there is much less published research focused on the organizational change process as a key ingredient leading to the ultimate success of community policing initiatives (Zhao, Thurman & Lovrich, 1995; Glensor & Peak, 1996). Here the organizational change literature suggests that for community policing to be successfully implemented and completely institutionalized, progress is needed inside law enforcement agencies in addition to the successes they achieve outside in the community.

This chapter highlights an innovative approach to promoting organizational change in policing that has worked for rural agencies in the western United States: the use of organizational and community assessments. This approach, which was developed by the Western Regional Institute for Community Oriented Public Safety (WRICOPS), provides law enforcement agencies with a way to objectively assess their organizational and external environment as they prepare themselves for change from a traditional to a community policing model.

Key Issues

The growing body of research in the area of organizational change to a community policing model suggests that change is not a simple process (Zhao, Thurman

& Lovrich, 1995; Glensor & Peak, 1996). These studies also suggest that the switch to community policing is affected by conditions both inside and outside the organization. For example, Zhao, Thurman, and Lovrich (1995) found that police officer training in the areas of ethics, police-community relations, and community policing principles were important developments necessary for the successful transition to a community policing model. And Peak and Glensor (1996) found that in addition to internal changes in management and leadership, community partnerships and problem solving were important as well if change was to occur inside the organization.

Many of these and other internal and external changes necessary for the success of community policing can be understood in terms of Jones's (1981) notion of an "organizational universe," a concept that drives the organizational and community assessment process pioneered by WRICOPS. This universe encompasses the organization and the relationships it generates both inside and outside the agency. According to this perspective, an organization is most effective when there is a close fit between five dimensions of the organizational universe. These five dimensions include: (1) organizational values, (2) organizational goals, (3) structure, (4) climate, and (5) community environment (Jones, 1981; WRICOPS, 1998).

Organizational Values and Organizational Goals

Organizational values typically associated with community policing include problem solving, community partnerships, and an emphasis on customer service. Organizational goals, on the other hand, result from the articulation of a department's values. Goals describe what outcomes a department wants to achieve (WRICOPS, 1998).

One of the basic elements of the organizational change process is strategic planning, an ongoing process by which organizations develop values and a mission, ultimately framing organizational goals, objectives, and operational strategies reflective of a community policing philosophy (Denhardt, 1995). A good fit between organizational values and goals is crucial for the strategic planning process.

Strategic planning necessarily involves all organizational employees (as well as other key stakeholders) in the process of planning organizational goals, objectives, and action plans. In addition, strategic planning typically attempts to predict how the work environment will change over a five- to ten-year period. Many departments across the United States that have adopted the community policing philosophy either have undertaken or are in the process of the often cumbersome task of strategic planning. And while many critics of strategic planning suggest that strategic planning is difficult and inefficient (as compared with a top-down approach to planning), the benefits of the process outweigh the pain.

Structure

Organizational structure is another dimension of the organizational universe (Jones, 1981). Major areas of structure that need to be examined prior to or during the organizational change process include the reporting and communication systems, rewards, accountability mechanisms, shift assignments, and management of calls for service. An organization's structural elements must fit with the agency's organizational values and goals in order for the organization to be effective (Jones, 1981; WRICOPS, 1998).

Several scholars have noted the importance of changes in structural elements in order for community policing to succeed. For example, Sparrow (1988) maintains that organizational communication is extremely important during the change process, and leaders in the organization not only need to "preach" the values of the department, but also must practice them in their daily actions. Denhardt (1995) maintains that participative management strategies, such as quality circles, are an ideal way not only to enhance communication within an organization, but also to allow employees at all levels of the organization to have some input into the change process (Denhardt, 1995).

Reward systems that promote community policing values and goals also have been considered important structural elements that lead to community policing success (Thurman, Zhao & Giacomazzi, 2001). Wycoff and Oettmeier (1994:3), who were involved in the Houston Police Department's creation of an experimental performance evaluation process designed to support community policing, note that employee performance evaluations should meet the following standards:

- Validity—Does the evaluation accurately reflect job content and expected quality of work?

- Reliability—Does the evaluation result in similar job performances being given similar evaluation ratings even if the actual evaluators are different people? Will similar job performances across time by the same employee result in similar evaluation ratings?

- Equity—Do employees who do the same or similar work receive equal evaluations of their performance?

- Legality—Are the evaluation results used to determine rewards and/or punishments for employees? If so, to what extent does the evaluation reflect the performance of an employee?

- Utility—Is there an underlying purpose for evaluating an employee's performance?

At the Houston Police Department, the experimental performance evaluation instruments assessed officers' performance from a variety of perspectives, including officers' immediate supervisors and citizens who were served by the police.

Climate

The climate of an organization stems from its implementation of structural elements (Jones, 1981; WRICOPS, 1998). The climate is composed of the unwritten rules and assumptions that drive organizational behavior, such as resistance to change, trust, role clarification, conflict, power issues, and informal communications. According to Jones (1981), a poor fit between an organization's values, goals, and structure is likely to produce an unhealthy organizational climate.

One typically mentioned obstacle to community policing is the traditional police culture. And while the traditional police culture is comprised of many elements, of particular importance here are the elements concerning the value that police officers in traditional organizations place on the role of citizens in the policing process. Quite simply, community policing suggests that citizens are equal partners with the police in the effort to improve the quality of their neighborhood life. The idea that police officers work with citizens in an effort to solve neighborhood problems is contrary to the traditional idea that the police are the experts and that citizens should do little more than serve as witnesses to crimes and report these incidents whenever they happen (Thurman, Zhao & Giacomazzi, 2001).

A successful transition to community policing depends on a climate in which the participation of other service providers and citizens as problem-solving partners is valued by the police. But changing culture is challenging. While many departments have successfully changed mission and values statements to reflect community policing ideals, the statements by themselves do little in the way of actually changing cultural beliefs. Important "structural" components can encourage a climate that is more conducive to community policing. For example, communicating an organization's mission and values, leading by example, implementing training initiatives, emphasizing the value of police-community partnerships, and publicizing behaviors consistent with the philosophy of community policing are just some of the ways that police leaders are beginning to deal with the cultural resistance to community policing. Several departments actively attempt to recruit and select police officers who embrace community policing ideals. For example, during a recent recruiting drive, the Portland (Oregon) Police Bureau emphasized its community orientation: "Become a Community Police Officer With the Portland Police Bureau! Our mission is to work with all citizens to preserve life, maintain human rights, protect property and promote individual responsibility and community commitment" (Portland Police Bureau, 1998).

But despite the obstacles to change, the successful transition to community policing depends on the ability of police leaders and employees to foster an organizational climate that supports continual learning, self-critique, and change (Geller, 1997).

Community Environment

Effective organizations learn to connect with their environments in meaningful ways. Citizen groups, the media, politicians, the business community, and other service providers can and should be involved in implementing community policing (WRICOPS, 1998). In fact, the input and participation of all key external stakeholders tends to imply an idea of police-community collaboration that is central to the success of community policing (DiIulio, 1993; Glensor & Peak, 1996).

John DiIulio (1993) shows that the role of citizens in the police process is far greater than simply reporting crimes to the police. DiIulio suggests that it is unrealistic for law enforcement to have a measurable positive impact on the quality of neighborhood life without the active assistance, cooperation, and participation of residents formally outside of government. In this relatively new spirit of community-police collaboration, the older ideas that judges, prosecutors, or the police could and should solve society's problems without the assistance of citizens is unrealistic. DiIulio notes that citizens have a large role in ensuring that justice is done, in promoting safe communities, in restoring victims of crime, and in promoting noncriminal options for offenders.

But if community policing is to succeed, citizens must assume responsibility for the quality of their neighborhood life. The question, however, is how this will happen. Oakes (1995) suggests that citizen responsibility can be encouraged by making positive examples more visible through rewards or media coverage. In addition, Oakes suggests a renewed emphasis on responsibility-building in the institutions that promote moral development, such as churches, schools, and family. And persistence among police organizations to embrace key stakeholders in communities by making them "partners" in the problem-solving process likely will lead to greater participation as well.

Toward Effective Implementation of Change

WRICOPS makes use of the organizational universe concept as the basis for its on-site assessment and as a model for structuring the assessment report. Such on-site organizational and community assessments are viewed as an effective means toward change in the public sector (see Vinzant & Vinzant, 1996).

The Western Regional Institute for Community Oriented Public Safety

The Office of Community Oriented Policing Services (COPS) is the federal office responsible for advancing community policing, including the addition of 100,000 community policing officers. COPS promotes community policing through a variety of initiatives, including its Regional Community Policing Institute (RCPI) program. WRICOPS is one such program, which services the northwestern United States, including Idaho, Montana, South Dakota, Washington, and Wyoming. As such, WRICOPS represents a partnership among Washington State University, the Washington Association of Sheriffs and Police Chiefs, and the Criminal Justice Training Commissions/Peace Officer Standards and Training organizations of its member states (WRICOPS, 1998).

The WRICOPS mission is to further the implementation of community policing via a threefold approach: training, applied research, and technical assistance (WRICOPS, 1998). WRICOPS' *training initiatives* are provided by a network of specifically trained and certified instructors from the region who provide instruction on a variety of topics, including problem solving and strategic planning. *Applied research* is provided in the form of organizational and community surveys designed to evaluate the effectiveness of community policing efforts to determine police and community perceptions of community policing and measure willingness to support community policing efforts, and to assess the a community's level of social capital. WRICOPS' *technical assistance* initiative, the primary focus of its outreach and the subject of this chapter, comes in the form of an on-site organization and community assessment related to community policing (WRICOPS, 1998).

Organizational Assessments as a Tool to Promote Change

The WRICOPS on-site assessment process is a comprehensive and innovative means to promote organizational change. It is designed to identify elements of both the internal and external environment that affect change. As such, the assessment process charts the current state of community policing within an agency, assesses understanding and support of community policing by employees, citizens, and local government, and determines attitudes about community policing from external stakeholders (WRICOPS, 1998).

WRICOPS draws from a pool of approximately 60 trained volunteers (leadership cadre members) who make themselves available to conduct assessments periodically. Prior to their first assessment, leadership cadre members attend a three-day workshop where they learn about the WRICOPS mission and are trained in interviewing and observation techniques. Ordinarily, five to eight cadre members comprise an individual assessment team, depending on the size of the department and other relevant issues (WRICOPS, 1998).

During the assessment, the leadership cadre spends approximately five days on-site collecting data, which typically includes the gathering of information from a variety of sources, including meetings, surveys, interviews, and observations. The on-site assessment process concludes with an exit interview with the chief or sheriff. Here, the leadership cadre team leader outlines findings and strategic recommendations designed to assist with the implementation of community policing. Typically, within three months a final report is issued to the organization's leading executive (WRICOPS, 1998).

To prepare for an assessment, leadership cadre members are asked to review a variety of documents prior to arriving on site. These documents typically include the agency's mission, annual reports, organizational chart, newspaper articles, training documents, etc. Once on site, the leadership cadre spends much of its time interviewing internal and external stakeholders using three different questionnaires: one for law enforcement, one for local government representatives, and one for community members. These questionnaires serve as a guide to ensure that many important topic areas—both inside and outside the department—are covered during the interviews. These topics include the following: understanding what community policing means; the vision/mission of the organization; the roles of chief executive, command staff, and first-line supervisors; organizational structure; union/association-related issues; calls for service management; management and planning services; human resources; budget; community partnerships; resistance/barriers to change; organizational communication patterns; issues of power/control; role of local government; internal/external relations; and social capital issues (WRICOPS, 1998).

To date, WRICOPS has conducted 21 on-site assessments throughout its five-state region. The assessment sites have included the following:

- Pierre, South Dakota, Police Department
- Casper, Wyoming, Police Department
- Nampa, Idaho, Police Department
- Douglas County, Washington, Sheriff's Office
- Helena, Montana, Police Department

Do Organizational Assessments Work?

WRICOPS' first assessment was conducted in a county sheriff's office in March 1998. This particular sheriff's office is responsible for the delivery of police patrol services to the outlying rural areas of its county, including two small towns. One of the towns has a current estimated population of 7,000, and the other is approximately 3,000 people.

The sheriff's office is staffed with 418 personnel, of which 213 are commissioned deputies. Personnel are assigned to one of four divisions—security, detective, patrol, or administration. In addition to providing law enforcement services for the unincorporated areas of the county and to its contract cities, it also provides regional jail service and regional dispatch services (WRICOPS, 1998).

For this assessment, the WRICOPS' on-site cadre members included two sheriffs, one police chief, one city mayor, a chamber of commerce president, an organizational development specialist, and the director of WRICOPS.

Approximately 75 interviews were conducted over five days, including interviews with 35 law enforcement officers and command staff and personnel from neighboring police departments. Fifteen local government officials were contacted, including the mayors of the sheriff's office's contract cities. City council members, county commissioners, judges, and prosecutors also were interviewed. Other respondents included local residents, school officials, school board members, neighborhood watch members, community representatives, business owners, and civic organization leaders (WRICOPS, 1998).

The WRICOPS' report called for organizational changes consistent with a community policing, including the decentralization of command authority, training focused on community policing, clarification of deputy roles under a community policing philosophy, and the development of new performance guidelines. A key recommendation of the assessment was that the sheriff's office should "strive to provide a personalized version for communities and areas that define themselves as communities"(WRICOPS, 1998:32).

The on-site assessment report outlined recommendations in 26 categories that encompassed the "organizational universe" in an effort to move the county sheriff's office closer to a broad implementation of community policing within the organization. One year after the release of the report, an evaluation team went back to the sheriff's office to determine progress. Based on data collected from observations, personal interviews, and a command staff focus group, the team noted several changes. Only those changes that all agreed had changed are listed below:

Values

There has been a change in department attitudes and values to become more "customer" oriented. Concerted efforts have been made to help people and increase police activity on "service" calls, such as disturbances, runaways, and lock-outs.

Goals

- Formal strategic planning efforts have commenced with an emphasis on identifying organizational goals.

Structure

- Deputies are now required to be involved in at least one problem-solving project.

- Raises and promotions are based in large part on community policing activities.

- Information is now solicited throughout the ranks of individual sections on what is needed in the budget, what changes should be made in the department, etc. Command staff considers this input and then makes decisions.

- There is a change in philosophy with regard to the hiring process. The organization is looking for self-starters and persons who can connect with the community.

- Patrol boundaries and assignments have changed as a result of the WRICOPS visit. Officers are now assigned to one area for 18 months.

- Deputies assigned to the contract cities are viewed as "part of the community."

- There is a sense that a militaristic model of policing has largely been broken down within the organization, while creativity is increasingly being celebrated and fostered. There is a sense that officers have the authority "to take the ball and run with it."

Climate

- While the community policing philosophy has existed in the organization, largely under the surface, WRICOPS helped bring it into reality and place it in writing.

- Deputies are now allowed to spend as much time on a call as needed to sufficiently deal with a particular problem.

- Problem solving, decentralization of officers, and community input have improved and expanded subsequent to WRICOPS participation.

- At a sheriff's office contract site at a local university, more officers are getting out of cars, and operations have changed in the sense that there is more emphasis on foot and bike patrols.

Community Environment

- Public participation has increased, especially in the contract cities, where there is considerable involvement in problem solving and support for the agency.

- There has been an increase in media releases—especially relating to community policing activities.

Discussion and Conclusion

One innovative way of examining a police agency's internal and external environment is through the use of organizational and community assessments. Using Jones's (1981) concept of the organizational universe as a framework for assessment, law enforcement agencies—both large and small—can examine both facilitators and barriers to change, and with a well-coordinated effort, can move toward organizational change to community policing.

A case in point is the county sheriff's office that was assessed on-site. An assessment team determined that the process resulted in positive change toward community policing and provided the sheriff's office with a road map for future change efforts. At the very least, the assessment accomplished the difficult task of changing the mindset of many agency employees and external stakeholders to embrace a favorable image of community policing. Furthermore, many of the personnel from the sheriff's office viewed the assessment as a seed-planting operation. While the sheriff's office had committed its organization to the philosophy of community policing prior to the assessment, the assessment cadre was credited with helping the department achieve significant progress in actually becoming a community policing organization.

While some have argued that the organizational change process to community policing takes longer in larger organizations (Glensor & Peak, 1996), this should not minimize the considerable time and effort that is needed to achieve police change in rural America. Whether an organization is large or small, community policing represents a challenging philosophical and operational shift. Law enforcement agencies intent on moving from a more traditional policing approach or agencies looking to broaden their community policing efforts from a specialized-unit approach will need to examine their organizations' internal and external environments and institute incremental changes if community policing is to take hold.

References

Chicago Community Policing Evaluation Consortium (1997). *Community Policing in Chicago, Year Four: Interim Report.* Illinois Criminal Justice Information Authority.

Denhardt, R. (1995). *Public Administration: An Action Orientation,* Second Edition. Belmont, CA: Wadsworth Publishing.

DiIulio, J.J. (1993). "Rethinking the Criminal Justice System: Toward a New Paradigm." In *Performance Measures for the Criminal Justice System, Discussion Papers from the BJS-Princeton Project.* Washington, DC: Office of Justice Programs, U.S. Department of Justice.

Geller, W.A. (1997). "Suppose We Were Really Serious About Police Departments Becoming Learning Organizations?" *National Institute of Justice Journal* (December):2-7.

Giacomazzi, A.L., R. Helms, and D. Brody (2000). "The Use of Organizational Assessments to Facilitate Change in Policing: An Evaluation of a Regional Community Policing Institute." A paper prepared for presentation at the 37th annual meeting of The Academy of Criminal Justice Sciences, New Orleans, Louisiana, March.

Jones, J.E. (1981). "The Organizational Universe," *1981 Annual Handbook for Group Facilitators.* San Diego, CA: University Associates.

McGarrell, E., S. Benitez, and R. Gutierrez (1997). "Getting to Know Your Community Through Citizen Surveys and Focus Group Interviews." In Q. Thurman and E. McGarrell (eds.), *Community Policing in a Rural Setting.* Cincinnati, OH: Anderson Publishing Co.

Peak, K.J. and R.W. Glensor (1996). *Community Policing and Problem Solving: Strategies and Practices.* Upper Saddle River, NJ: Prentice Hall.

Oakes, D.H. (1995). "Rights and Responsibilities." In Amitai Etzioni (ed.), *Rights and the Common Good: The Communitarian Perspective.* New York, NY: St. Martin's Press.

Office of Community Oriented Policing Services (2000). http://www.usdoj.gov/cops/.

Portland Police Bureau (1998). Recruiting flyer, November 1998.

Roberg, R., J. Crank, and J. Kuykendall (2000). *Police and Society.* Los Angeles, CA: Roxbury Publishing Company.

Reisig, M.D., and R.B. Parks (2000). "Experience, Quality of Life, and Neighborhood Context: A Hierarchical Analysis of Satisfaction with Police." *Justice Quarterly* 17(3):607-630.

Reiss, A. (1971). *The Police and the Public.* New Haven, CT: Yale University Press.

Sparrow, M.K. (1988). "Implementing Community Policing," *Perspectives on Policing*, November 1988. Washington, DC: Office of Justice Programs, U.S. Department of Justice.

Thurman, Q.T., J. Zhao, and A.L. Giacomazzi (2001). *Community Policing in a Community Era: An Introduction and Exploration.* Los Angeles, CA: Roxbury Publishing Company.

Vinzant, D.H., and J.C. Vinzant (1996). "Strategy and Organizational Capacity: Finding a Fit." *Public Productivity and Management Review* Vol. 20 (2):139-157.

WRICOPS (1998). *Community Policing Assessment Report: County Sheriff's Office.* Western Regional Institute for Community Oriented Public Safety.

Wycoff, M.A., and T. Oettmeier (1994). *Evaluating Patrol Officer Performance Under Community Policing: The Houston Experience.* National Institute of Justice Research Report. Washington, DC: Office of Justice Programs, U.S. Department of Justice.

Zhao, J., Q.C. Thurman, and N.P. Lovrich (1995). "Community-Oriented Policing Across the U.S.: Facilitators and Impediments to Implementation." *American Journal of Police* 14:11-28.

The Work Routines and Citizen Interactions of Small-Town and Rural Police Officers　　6

James Frank
University of Cincinnati

John Liederbach
University of North Texas

Introduction

The workload of police officers has been the focus of a number of studies during the past 30 years.[1] Using a variety of research methodologies, from examining calls to the police and dispatch records to observational studies, this research has focused on providing an understanding of the types of activities police officers perform on a daily basis (Cordner, 1978; Cumming, Cumming & Edell, 1965; Frank, Brandl & Watkins, 1997; Greene & Klockars, 1991; Kelling, Pate, Dieckman & Brown, 1974; O'Neill & Bloom, 1972; Reiss, 1971; Webster, 1970; Wilson, 1968; Parks, Mastrofski, DeJong & Gray, 1999). Unfortunately, most, if not all, of this research describes the work routines of officers employed by large police agencies.

Recently, however, there has been increasing interest in the practices of smaller police agencies, and especially rural and small-town police organizations (Maguire et al., 1997; Thurman & McGarrell, 1997; Weisheit, Falcone & Wells, 1996; Weisheit, Wells & Falcone; 1994; Crank, 1990). For instance, Weisheit et al. (1996), using data collected through focus groups, in-person interviews, and surveys, suggest that rural and small-town policing is quite different from policing performed in large urban departments. Using primarily anecdotal evidence, they contend that officers are more connected to their communities, handle a wide range of community problems that are not law enforcement issues, and are oriented to problem solving more so than just responding to criminal incidents. Similarly, Thurman and McGarrell (1997) note that small-town police are more service oriented and perform much fewer law enforcement activities than do urban police

---

[1]　The work in this chapter was supported by the National Institute of Justice, grant number 98-IJ-CX-0063. Points of view are those of the authors and do not necessarily represent the view of the U.S. Department of Justice or the National Institute of Justice.

officers. Meagher (1985), using data collected through a task analysis questionnaire, found that officers in small departments were less likely to perform tasks involving traffic accidents, investigations of suspicious activities, criminal incidents, and the preparation of formal reports. Finally, studies exploring officer perceptions of their work environment (Winfree, Guiterman & Mays, 1997) and officer beliefs about public support (Kowalewski, Hall, Dolan & Anderson, 1984), determined that officers in smaller departments perceived more public support and respect than did officers working in larger agencies.

What this expanding body of knowledge has failed to do, however, is provide systematic information on how policing is accomplished in small police organizations, especially rural and small-town departments. The result is that there exists only a limited body of empirical information about the actual tasks and workload of officers employed by smaller law enforcement agencies, the nature of interactions these officers have with citizens and, apart from anecdotal information, whether small police departments are actually performing community policing.

The lack of empirical data regarding how policing is accomplished in smaller agencies is especially troubling given the current movement emphasizing community policing strategies, advocates of which imply that officers should perform specific activities consistent with that philosophy. Coupled with this is the fact that many contend that "community policing looks and sounds a great deal like rural and small-town policing, as it has been practiced for a long time." (Weisheit et al., 1994:551). Thurman and McGarrell (1997:9) stated that many small-town and rural police "insist that community-oriented policing is what they have always done."

To what degree does community policing already reflect the practices and experiences of officers who work in rural and small-town agencies? Weisheit and his associates (1996, 1994) determined that small-town police were knowledgeable about community norms, more connected to their communities, and oriented to problem-solving activities. Officers in small departments were determined to be better known by citizens (Ostrom & Smith, 1976), were more responsive to preventive patrol and proactive policing (Meagher, 1985), and were more responsive to the demands of their constituents (Crank, 1990; Kowalewski et al., 1984; Wilson, 1968). Moreover, small police organizations appear to generate more personal relationships among officers, as well as between officers and their communities (Langworthy & Travis, 2003). Maguire and his associates (1997), in their study of community policing in nonurban areas (populations of 50,000 or less), reported that most of these agencies performed a wide range of community policing activities, although these tasks were performed to a greater degree by large departments in their sample. Still, to more definitively assess whether community policing is performed in rural and small departments, it is necessary to systematically examine what officers do when they take on community policing responsibilities.

Key Issues

Community policing is the current watchword in policing and has become "the dominant strategy of policing" (Cordner, 1997:45; see also Rosenbaum & Lurigio, 1994; Eck & Rosenbaum, 1994). While police administrators and researchers continue the debate over what this strategy entails and how it is to be implemented, several common themes run throughout the various definitions. The major themes are increased interaction between police and citizens, increased citizen input, and responses tailored to specific community needs and desires (Alpert & Moore, 1993; Goldstein, 1987; Reiss & Tonry, 1986; Skolnick & Bayley, 1987; Webb & Katz, 1997). Essentially, community police officers should engage in more service and order-maintenance activities than law enforcement activities (Kratcoski & Dukes, 1995; Mastrofski, Worden & Snipes, 1995).

In order to assess whether rural and small-town police agencies are performing community policing, it is important to examine the tasks and activities that officers of these departments perform during their typical work shift. This information will provide evidence regarding what Cordner (1997) describes as the "Tactical Dimension" of community policing. Specifically, this chapter addresses two critical issues:

What tasks and activities do officers in rural, small-town, and suburban law enforcement agencies perform during their typical work day?

What is the nature of interactions that police officers have with citizens and non-police service providers during their work shifts?

The findings reported here are derived from data collected using systematic social observations of police officers in 11 southwestern Ohio police departments. This data is part of a larger project that includes observational data from 10 additional small agencies that were excluded from the current analysis because their jurisdictions are contiguous to and/or surrounded by a large urban center. Of the 11 departments included in this analysis, four are rural municipal police agencies. Each of these agencies employs a limited number of officers (2-7) and serves populations under 2,500. More importantly, the areas served by these agencies are physically isolated from both an urban center and any concentrated residential areas. One additional agency is a rural sheriff's department. Also included in the analysis is one small-town municipal agency. This police department serves a population of 9,000 people, employs 20 officers, and the police jurisdiction is approximately 20 miles from an urban center. Two departments have been categorized as transitional small-town agencies. Twenty years ago, the sites would have likely been classified in the small-town rural category, but each has since undergone rapid population growth and residential home construction. One of these transitional small-town agencies now serves a population of 10,000, while the other city has approximately 6,000 inhabitants. The remaining three sites are commercialized suburban agencies and serve areas that are on the periphery of an urban center. Each serves mixed communities comprised of major retailing outlets (malls and shopping centers), limited heavy industry, and core residential areas. These three police departments have more diverse demands on their time in comparison to the other study agencies, largely due to an influx of both workers and consumers that significantly increases their daytime populations.

The data were collected through systematic observations of officers that were performed during 30 randomly selected shifts in each of the 11 police agencies. All observers were initially trained on accepted observation techniques. Observers were instructed to collect information concerning the nature of each activity observed and to account for every minute the officer was on duty. As such, data were collected on the amount of time spent on each observed activity (e.g., driving to community meetings, preparing administrative reports, assisting citizens, investigating crimes, meals, personal time, routine patrol, performing non-police tasks) and the characteristics of each activity (e.g., complainant, whether the activity involved problem solving, who initiated the activity, and other situational characteristics). Observers also collected data on all face-to-face interactions (e.g., service-related, friendly conversations between acquaintances, etc.) between police officers and citizens and/or public service providers employed by agencies external to their police department (characteristics of citizens, who initiates the interaction, the nature of the interaction).

Findings

Findings concerning the behavior of rural and small-town officers are presented using two separate categories of observational data. The first category, "activities," consists of duties officers perform when they are not in the presence of citizens. This category also includes instances in which citizens were present but no verbal or physical exchange between officer and citizen took place (Parks et al., 1999). Officer "activities" include, but are not limited to, duties such as motorized patrol, administrative assignments, non-police tasks, and a wide array of traditional police functions performed outside the purview of citizens. These findings are presented in terms of the percent of total "activity" minutes (i.e., time spent *not* interacting with citizens) consumed across various types of activities. The second category of data, "encounters," includes all face-to-face contacts with citizens. Encounters may involve verbal exchanges between officer and citizen, as well as physical contacts (Parks et al., 1999).

Officer Activities

The observed rural and small-town officers clearly spend the vast majority of their time performing tasks that do not involve citizen contact. On average, the observed officers spent less than 17 percent of their shift interacting with citizens, or 81.6 minutes of an eight-hour shift. This finding was consistent across the five small agency types, ranging from slightly less than 14 percent in the transitional small-town agencies and reaching 20 percent in the commercialized suburban agencies. The predominance of "activity" time may be most clearly illustrated in terms of the typical eight-hour shift. Our observed officers spent an average of more than six and one-half hours per shift either by themselves or with other officers.

What do rural and small-town officers do when they are not interacting with citizens? We examine this issue in terms of the amount of time that these officers spend performing various categories of "activities," or tasks that do not involve contact with citizens. Motorized patrol is the most frequent activity performed by our observed rural and small-town officers. Officers across the 11 agencies spent an average of more than 37 percent of their time away from citizens performing motorized patrol. In fact, officers employed by the two transitional small-town agencies spent an average of more than 41 percent of all activity time on patrol. None of the 11 agencies spent less than 30 percent of their activity time performing patrol duties.

The remainder of officer activity time is dominated by three other tasks—administrative duties (e.g., report writing, automobile maintenance), non-police tasks (e.g., personal business, breaks, meals), and driving to and from specific destinations. These three activities combined to consume an average of more than 44 percent of total activity time, with administrative activities accounting for slightly more than 20 percent, non-police tasks consuming slightly less than 13 percent, and driving 11 percent. Activity time spent on administrative duties ranged from a low of 14 percent for the rural county sheriff department to a high of more than 22 percent for the four rural municipal agencies. These officers also seem to spend a significant percentage of time performing non-police tasks. For example, observed officers in the rural or small-town agency spent more than 15 percent of their activity time doing such things as personal errands or taking breaks.

While these 11 agencies appear to be similar in the degree to which they perform motorized patrol, administrative duties, and non-police tasks, there were striking differences in the range of time spent en route to specific destinations. For example, officers observed in the rural county sheriff's department spent more than twice as much time en route (21%) as did their municipal counterparts who patrol in the identical county (8%), a finding that clearly illustrates the differences in jurisdictional sizes among rural municipal and rural sheriff's departments.

The activity time consumed by other activities such as criminal matters, service-related functions, and order maintenance tasks appears to be surprisingly small (approximately 19%). However, these low percentages must be viewed in light of the distinction between "activity" and "encounter" time. That is, much of the time officers spend dealing with criminal matters, service duties, and order-maintenance activities necessarily, by their very nature, involve some type of citizen interaction, and are thereby discussed in the following section on citizen encounters.

Citizen Encounters

In addition to providing an examination of how rural and small-town officers spend their time away from citizens, observational data allows a unique opportunity to describe the ways in which police officers interact with, or "encounter," citizens on the job. Consistent with previous observation literature (see Parks et al., 1999), our observers differentiated police/citizen encounters into three distinct categories. *Full* encounters occupy at least one minute of the observed officer's time or involve three or more exchanges of words or gestures. Full encounters must also involve police business. *Brief* encounters also involve police business, but occupy less than one minute of time. In contrast, *casual* encounters do not involve police business. Given the degree to which various factors outside the officer's control may influence the amount of time spent on individual citizen encounters (e.g., offense seriousness, time of day, weather conditions), our encounter findings present each individual encounter as a percentage of the total number of citizen encounters for each observed agency.

The findings reveal substantial variation across small agency types in terms of the three categories of citizen encounters described above. For example, the rural county sheriff's department and the commercialized suburban agencies featured a greater percentage of full encounters (73% and 67% respectively) than did the remainder of the sample. Moreover, these agency types were much less likely than the rest of the sample to have had casual encounters with citizens (2.5% and 8.8% respectively). In contrast, casual encounters were most prevalent among the rural municipal agencies (17%). These differences may reflect variations in both the occupational duties and community demographics *within* the class of smaller police agencies—a factor often ignored in previous literature.

Beyond simply classifying police-citizen encounters by type, observational data may be used to further describe the nature and characteristics of these encounters; that is, the process by which police officers come to interact with citizens and the problems that police are expected to handle once they encounter them. To this end, we next turn our attention to the ways in which officers employed by these smaller agencies were "mobilized" to interact with citizens. First, our observed officers initiated the greatest percentage of encounters by themselves (48%). The second most prevalent form of mobilization was dispatch (31%). Together, these two categories account for more than three-fourths of all mobilizations that resulted in citizen encounters. Supervisors, other officers, and citizens (both on-scene and by telephone) accounted for the balance of the mobilizations.

Again, the data reveal considerable variation in the source of mobilization across small agency types. For example, rural municipal agencies displayed the greatest percentage of citizen mobilizations (24%), possibly reflecting the degree to which citizens living in rural communities may feel more connected to the police than citizens from more populous localities. This finding is underscored by the fact that observed officers employed by commercialized suburban agencies were mobilized by dispatch (41%) to a greater degree than any of the other four small agency groups. Finally, observed county sheriff's deputies were more than twice as likely to be mobilized by supervisors (14%) than their municipal counterparts. This finding can, at least in part, be attributed to the task of serving warrants—a duty most often relegated to county sheriff's departments.

Once mobilized to the scene of a citizen encounter, police officers can be expected to confront a wide range of problems upon their arrival. These "problems" denote the underlying reason for the police officer's presence, and as such, are one way to describe the nature of police-citizen interactions in smaller jurisdictions. Observers identified the underlying problem in every observed encounter using more than 200 individual problem codes. These codes were collapsed into eight more readily identifiable groups including crime-related matters, order maintenance, traffic, service, administrative problems, ordinance enforcement, information gathering, and problem solving.

In terms of crime-related problems, a distinction can again be made between the rural county sheriff's department and the 10 other smaller municipal agencies. More than one-half of all the problems handled by the sheriff's deputies (54%) were crime-related, while crime-related problems were much less prevalent in the rural municipal agencies (31%), the rural small-town department (25%), the commercialized suburban agencies (30%), and the transitional small-town departments (29%).

A significant number of problems handled by these 11 agencies involve traffic (slightly more than 30% on average); however, the prevalence of traffic-related problems fluctuates greatly among these agencies depending, at least in part, on the existence of major traffic arteries or interstates within these jurisdictions. For example, traffic problems account for almost 43 percent of the problems confronted by the rural small town due to the presence of a major interstate highway and numerous semitrailer weigh stations. In contrast, one of the rural municipal agencies encounters a very limited number of traffic problems (8%) because the jurisdiction is comprised of little more than one two-lane thoroughfare surrounded by a small, sparsely populated rural area.

Service-related issues are the third most prevalent problem type confronted by these agencies (slightly more than 20% on average). The prevalence of service-related problems ranges from a high of 26 percent in the commercialized suburban agencies and a low of 12 percent for the rural county sheriff's department. Again, this difference may be attributed to variations within a group of agencies that have often been generically termed simply as "small" in previous studies. Specifically, officers employed by the commercialized suburban agencies often perform tasks such as vehicle lock-outs, giving directions, or responding to commercial alarms— problems more closely associated with the cosmopolitan nature of growing suburban cities. In contrast, these duties are more rare for the rural county sheriff's department because they are often performed by the rural municipal agencies contained within their jurisdiction.

Another critical aspect that contributes to an understanding of the character of police and citizen interactions in smaller agencies involves the degree to which these officers are familiar with the citizens whom they encounter. This issue is especially salient in the era of community policing, which has focused attention on the need to foster stronger links between officers, the communities they police, and the citizens they serve. Among our sampled agencies, the rural municipal departments were much more likely to know the citizens they encountered "very well" (18% of all citizens) than the other small agency types (slightly more than 6% on average). As prior literature suggests, officers who work in small, rural communities appear to be more connected to citizens and more likely to form strong social ties to the communities they serve.

Discussion

This chapter represents an attempt to: (1) identify the types of activities performed by small-town and rural police officers, (2) identify the amount of time officers spend on these activities, and (3) to describe the nature and characteristics of the interactions these officers have with citizens they encounter. These research tasks were intended to systematically examine the work routine of officers and assess whether officers in smaller agencies are performing community policing.

First, it appears that the work of officers in our study sites varies across several of the agency types. The rural, transitional, and small-town agency categories exhibited the greatest degree of consistency in terms of officer activities and citizen encounters. The work of these agencies appears to differ from that of the rural county sheriff's department, as well as the commercialized suburban agencies. As such, for our agencies at least, rural and small-town departments should not be seen as unitary entities. For example, our sheriff's department was more likely than other agencies to be involved in full encounters that were crime-related and less likely to be involved in interactions that concerned the provision of services. Both the sheriff and the commercialized suburban officers were less likely than the rural agency officers to be familiar with the people with whom they interacted. While it was not the intention to determine the cause of the variation across agency categories, it is likely that this variation results because of differences in population demographics and occupational mandates.

Second, many of our findings support the existing interview and anecdotal data on rural policing. Specifically, the rural and small-town agencies had more citizen contact, were more likely to be mobilized by citizens (versus dispatchers), and were more likely to know the citizens they encountered "very well" than the rural county sheriff's department and the commercialized suburban agencies. Furthermore, the findings relative to brief and casual encounters suggest that rural and small-town officers are more likely than other study officers to engage in non-adversarial exchanges with citizens. In general, officers in these departments are more likely to have informal interactions with people they know. This finding clearly supports the existing literature concerning the experience of policing rural communities (see esp. Weisheit et al., 1997), which suggests that the cultural conditions inherently found in these communities facilitates the formation of strong social ties (both on *and* off the job) between officers and citizens—an environment that naturally breeds more personal interactions. When these findings are taken together, it appears that these agencies, at least presently, are performing community policing activities.

Third, as far as officer activities are concerned, a couple of matters are worthy of further mention. Activities that consumed the greatest proportion of office time in workload research involving large departments (patrol, administrative tasks) also comprise a large portion of the work day of small-town and rural officers. Traffic-related work was also frequently performed by our officers. Thus, it appears that certain activities, by their very nature, are part of the work routine of people engaged in policing, irrespective of agency size and type. When officers act in the presence of citizens, however, there appear to be differences between the rural and small agencies in the types of citizens whom they encounter and the problems officers handle, because larger agencies tend to serve more heterogeneous populations. These issues remain for future empirical scrutiny.

Officer Activities

Activity	Percent	Minutes Per Shift (8-Hr.)	Minimum/Maximum
Motor Patrol	37.31	179.08	148.65/208.60
Administrative	20.83	99.98	68.92/157.96
Personal	12.95	62.16	41.56/92.35
En route/Waiting	11.04	52.99	28.89/101.18
Traffic	4.56	21.88	12.72/43.34
Crime	1.92	9.21	3.31/19.24
Order Maintenance	1.49	7.15	1.39/14.54
Service	1.38	6.62	1.63/12.62
Other	8.52	40.89	

Encounters by Type (%)

Agency Groups	Full Encounters	Brief Encounters	Casual Encounters
Rural County Sheriff	73.6	23.9	2.5
Rural Municipal	64.6	17.9	17.5
Rural Small-Town	64.9	21.8	13.4
Commercialized Suburban	67.1	24.1	8.8
Transitional Small-Town	53.8	32.5	3.7

References

Alpert, G.P., and M.H. Moore (1993). "Measuring Police Performance in the New Paradigm of Policing." In G. Alpert and A. Piquero (eds.), *Community Policing: Contemporary Readings*. Prospect Heights, IL: Waveland Press, Inc.

Cordner, G.W. (1997). "Community Policing: Elements and Effects." In R.G. Dunham and G.P. Alpert (eds.), *Critical Issues in Policing*, Third Edition. Prospect Heights, IL: Waveland Press, Inc.

Cordner, G. (1978). "While on Routine Patrol . . . : A Study of Police Use of Uncommitted Patrol Time." Unpublished Master's thesis. East Lansing, MI: School of Criminal Justice, Michigan State University.

Cordner, G., and K.E. Scarborough (1997). "Operationalizing Community Policing in Rural America: Sense and Nonsense." In Q.C. Thurman and E.F. McGarrell (eds.), *Community Policing in a Rural Setting*. Cincinnati, OH: Anderson Publishing Co.

Crank, J. (1990). "The Influence of Environmental and Organizational Factors on Police Style in Urban and Rural Police Departments." *Journal of Research in Crime and Delinquency* 27(2): 166-189.

Cumming, E., I. Cumming, and L. Edell (1965). "Policeman as a Philosopher, Friend and Guide." *Social Problems* 12:276-286.

Eck, J., and D. Rosenbaum (1994). "An Inside Look at Community Policing Reform: Definitions, Organizational Changes, and Evaluation Findings." *Crime & Delinquency* 40:299-314.

Frank, J., S. Brandl, and R.C. Watkins (1997). "The Content of Community Policing: A Comparison of the Daily Activities of Community and Beat Officers." *Policing: An International Journal of Police Strategies and Management* 20(4):716-728.

Goldstein, H. (1987). "Toward Community-Oriented Policing: Potential, Basic Requirements, and Threshold Questions." *Crime and Delinquency* 33:6-30.

Greene, J., and C. Klockars (1991). "What Police Do." In C. Klockars and S. Mastrofski (eds.), *Thinking About Police,* Second Edition. New York, NY: McGraw-Hill.

Kelling, G., T. Pate, D. Dieckman, and C. Brown (1974). *The Kansas City Preventive Patrol Experiment: A Summary Report.* Washington, DC: Police Foundation.

Kowalewski, D., W. Hall, J. Dolan, and J. Anderson (1984). "Police Environments and Operational Codes: A Case Study of Rural Settings." *Journal of Police Science and Administration* 12:363-372.

Kratcoski, P.C., and D. Dukes (1995). "Activity Time Allocations of Community Policing Officers." In P.C. Kratcoski and D. Dukes (eds.), *Issues in Community Policing.* Cincinnati, OH: Anderson Publishing Co.

Langworthy, R.H. and L.F. Travis (2003). *Policing in America: A Balance of Forces*, Third Edition. Upper Saddle River, NJ: Prentice Hall.

Maguire, E.R., J.B. Kuhns, C.D. Uchida, and S.M. Cox (1997). "Patterns of Community Policing in Nonurban America." *Journal of Research in Crime and Delinquency* 34(3):368-394.

Mastrofski, S.D., R.E. Worden, and J.B. Snipes (1995). "Law Enforcement in a Time of Community Policing." *Criminology* 33:539-563.

Meagher, M.S. (1985). "Police Patrol Styles: How Pervasive is Community Variation?" *Journal of Police Science and Administration* 13:36-45.

O'Neill, M., and C. Bloom (1972). "The Field Officer: Is He Really Fighting Crime?" *Police Chief* 39:30-32.

Ostrom, E., and D. Smith (1976). "On the Fate of 'Lilliputs' in Metropolitan Policing." *Public Administration Review* 36(2):192-200.

Parks, R., S. Mastrofski, C. DeJong, and M. Gray (1999). "How Officers Spend Their Time with the Community." *Justice Quarterly* 16:483-518.

Reiss, A.J. (1971). *The Police and the Public.* New Haven, CT: Yale University Press.

Reiss, A.J., and M. Tonry (eds.) (1986). *Communities and Crime.* Chicago, IL: University of Chicago Press.

Rosenbaum, D.P., and A.J. Lurigio (1994). "An Inside Look at Community Policing Reform: Definitions, Organizational Change, and Evaluation Findings." *Crime & Delinquency* 40:299-314.

Skolnick, J.H., and D.H. Bayley (1987). "Theme and Variation in Community Policing." In M. Tonry and N. Morris (eds.), *Crime and Justice.* Chicago, IL: University of Chicago Press.

Thurman, Q.C., and E. McGarrell (1997). *Community Policing in a Rural Setting.* Cincinnati, OH: Anderson Publishing Co.

Webb, V.J., and C.M. Katz (1997). "Citizen Ratings of the Importance of Community Policing Activities." *Policing: An International Journal of Police Strategies and Management* 20:7-23.

Webster, J.A. (1970). "Police Task and Time Study." *Journal of Criminal Law, Criminology, and Police Science* 61:94-100.

Weisheit, R., D. Falcone, and L.E. Wells (1996). *Crime and Policing in Rural and Small-Town America.* Prospect Heights, IL: Waveland Press, Inc.

Weisheit, R., and C.W. Hawkins (1997). "The State of Community Policing in Small Towns and Rural Areas." In Q.C. Thurman and E.F. McGarrell (eds.), *Community Policing in a Rural Setting.* Cincinnati, OH: Anderson Publishing Co.

Weisheit, R., L.E. Wells, and D. Falcone (1994). "Community Policing in Small-Town and Rural America." *Crime and Delinquency*, 40(4):549-567.

Wilson, J.Q. (1968). *Varieties of Police Behavior.* Cambridge, MA: Harvard University Press.

Winfree, T., D. Guiterman, and G.L. Mays (1997). "Work Assignments and Police Work: Exploring the World of Sworn Officers in Four New Mexico Police Departments." *Policing: An International Journal of Police Strategies and Management*, 20(2):419-441.

Zhao, J. (1996). *Why Police Organizations Change: A Study of Community-Oriented Policing.* Washington, DC: Police Executive Research Forum.

Celebrating Agency Culture: Engaging a Traditional Cop's Heart in Organizational Change 7

John P. Crank
Boise State University

Introduction

Police agency reform seldom occurs gracefully. Efforts to change police organizations will try the temper of even the most patient manager. Yet resistance to reform, thought to be ubiquitous to police organizations, is poorly understood.

What are the primary obstacles to reform? High on most reformer's lists are traditional officers and the police culture, also called the "blue shield." It is argued in this chapter that the police culture, carried by experienced officers, is where meaningful change can and must occur. Community-based reform can occur only when law enforcement executives overcome their traditional administrative distrust of its street officers and allow street-level skills and wisdom to be used on behalf of organizational change.

Key Issues

Reform and Street Wisdom

When I first began writing this chapter, I was presented with a suggested title that went something like "Overcoming Agency Culture." Implicit in this suggestion is a way of thinking about experienced police officers, a view I have seen shared by both academicians and police administrators, that police culture is a problem, a source of troubling resistance to change. This image reflects a prevailing and persistent tendency to blame police culture for all of the problems associated with the police—police secrecy, abuse of discretion, misuse of force, and so on.

It is also a wrong view. It is a conception of culture that is limited and one-dimensional. Culture is perceived to be a set of moral blinders that limit the ability of the police to fully appreciate the world around them. The "blinder" is a metaphor for their protective, secretive culture, and it keeps them focused only on protecting other officers and on CYA ("Cover Your Ass"), and prevents them from seeing and understanding the good that can come from change. If the blinders can be removed, if reformers can somehow figure out how to penetrate the secretive police culture, then true change can occur. But first the blinders have to be removed—culture has to be overcome.

Well, then, what is wrong with the blinder metaphor? There can be little debate that cops are sometimes secretive, an observation widely noted among both outsiders and cops themselves. But the blinder metaphor paints too dark an image of police culture. If the working environment of street cops were really this way, then why on earth would anyone ever want to be or remain a cop? Police work must be something more than a lonely encroaching cynical darkness of spirit, a continual adjustment to a frustrating task that contains few rewards, marked by boredom, CYA and, finally, retirement in northern Idaho.

The dark image of police work described above is certainly not held by street cops. When experienced veterans talk about their work, they rarely describe a barren image of their careers. They see themselves as having experienced a special life, different from citizens who spend their working days cloistered away in offices. They see the life of the civilian working stiff as boring, unanimated, incomplete. They have seen all that their community has to offer, not only the bad that is so widely cited by observers and researchers, but the good as well. They are part of its history. They carry a sense of battles won and lost, of profound accomplishment. To them the community is a blanket of interwoven threads, a living entity over which they have held dominion and to which they have given their hearts and souls.

Seasoned officers are culture carriers, the department's living traditions acted out daily. They have acquired a practical understanding about people on their beat. They know how to deal with them. They have "tool kits" of solutions to the everyday, garden-variety problems to which they are long accustomed. They have a sense of when to speak softly, when to use command voice, when to ignore, or when to look closer. They know the saturnine alleys, the quiet roads where lovers sneak away, the fields where teenagers go to drink on Saturday night, the safe havens, and the areas that need pressure. They chafe at the limits of their ability to respond to problems—to arrest bad guys, to provide activities for young people.

When community policing advocates complain about the impenetrable wall of silence and the entrenched resistance of line officers, they are often talking about the experienced officers described above. These officers, they say, already "know it all," they do not trust academics, and they just want to know specifics—how it helps them deal with crime. This is the wall with which community policing reform collides.

Reformers want to fix culture. But culture is much more than a set of blinders—it is a way of solving problems, of thinking about keeping the peace, of traditions, about life's celebrations. Culture carries the history and meanings of the organization in the acts and lives of its participants—it is agency experience acted out in the behavior of individual officers and shared among its members. It encompasses diverse skills and the knowledge about how and when to use them. It is steeped in moral rightness. It is a human celebration of "copness." It is not something to be fixed.

Seasoned officers have developed a way of looking at and responding to their working environment, a worldview that works. It is, as Manning (1977) has noted, a worldview that is fiercely individualistic, one of the last occupational frontiers of traditional values in a society undergoing troubling moral changes. It is intensely practical, honed on skills that have been applied time after time. It is surprisingly effective in dealing with the most difficult, unpredictable, and stubborn of all organizational products—human behavior. Problem-solving responsibility lies with individual cops, working alone, with back-up occasionally, sometimes with supportive citizens who, like them, have no truck for criminals and unsympathetic jerks. It is a profoundly moral outlook on the world, as Skolnick and Bayley (1986) have observed, a crime control mandate that at the street level is revealed in the ability of cops to maintain order on their beats.

I have heard chiefs lament that community-based reforms will have to wait until the resistant "old guard" dies out. What a loss this would be. The old guard carries the true knowledge of the department. These officers, not brass, and certainly not reformers, know how to do police work. If change is to be effective, if it is to be "sold" to the organization, it is to the old guard that it should be sold.

Consider Jack Wilson, a deputy in a sheriff's department in southwest Idaho. He has been with the department for 25 years. No longer a young man, he still brings to his work a vigor and energy than many men of lesser years have lost to a daily routine of television, the couch, and a six-pack and chips. His beat is a rural area by any standard. The largest community is about 30,000, and his patrol activity takes him there infrequently. He also keeps tabs on two very small communities of a few hundred each.

Wilson knows many citizens by name, where their parents are buried, where their children go to school. In one community, he stops to meet with a group of citizens who have formed a citizens' watch. There are about 30 people present; it appears to be one-half of the adult community. He knows them all by first name. They recently made "citizens' watch" sweatshirts and have them on today. A woman sends her son into a shack to get Wilson a cup of coffee as soon as he arrives. They hold him in high esteem; he is a prince to them. In another community, he meets with a family who are the stalwarts of a two-year citizen's band patrol. The patrol was initiated in response to a drug distribution center that was set up in this small community. They still talk about busting the operatives every time they see him. "Hey Jack, remember when . . . ?" And they reminisce over the fights, the chase, and the arrests. In another community, he looks at the old school and the playground. They need a basketball hoop. He knows that if he could somehow get the money to put up a hoop, then the kids of Hispanic migrants would have something to do and a safe place to do it. He is troubled by their lack of leisure activities and knows that some of them will get into trouble without other outlets.

Sometimes he takes his patrol car and searches out the obscure parts of the county. He enjoys the drive along the river best; it reminds him of hunting and fishing. And he does not have to imagine it from an office cubicle. He can drive by it, see it, smell it, even get out of his car and have lunch there if he wants. He can drive his patrol car down the highway and look out at an immense Idaho sunset. His work and his life flow together, make him what he is. He is the cultural heritage of his department.

What a waste it would be to the police and the public to view this officer as simply an "obstacle" to change. The skills, concrete knowledge, departmental traditions, communities served, practical sense of trouble spots, understanding of local problems, wide friendship networks—all that makes the job a human experience—would be lost. Reform is limited because it sees culture as a problem, and ends up viewing traditional cops—true culture carriers—as sources of resistance. Culture is misconceived as a cop problem. It is a human condition, carrier of celebration and grim tragedy, full of emotions and knowledge, life, meaning. If our goal is to overcome cop culture, we risk sacrificing cop humanity.

Discussion

Common Sense and Reform

If reformers want to be effective, reform must make sense, otherwise it will be rejected out of hand. Cops' commonsense ways of thinking and dealing with recurring problems is the binding force of police culture. Yet common sense has special meanings for the police. Some aspects of cop common sense are described below, together with their implications for police reform.

First, police are practical. Their skills and knowledge are rooted in everyday work. As Wilson (1968) once observed, they approach their work from the point of view of handling situations—an observation that applies more aptly to the concrete nature of police work than to its order-maintaining qualities. Their relations with citizens are worked out in concrete encounters, and their sense of those encounters—what worked and what did not, who did what, how things ended up—forms the body of their commonsense knowledge. They think practically; when asked to explain something, they will inevitably provide an example drawn from their practical lore of circumstances and people. Any effort to instill change must (1) make practical sense, and (2) provide cops with the opportunity to use their practical skills to deal with problems.

Second, police are pragmatic. They are interested in what works. Common sense has a pragmatism to it that cannot be learned apart from doing police work. An officer may learn, for example, how to put a set of cuffs on a suspect, but actually putting them on a citizen during an arrest is a different kind of knowledge, a sense of what people do and how they react when taken into custody. Change has to be conveyed in terms of its pragmatic effects on their behavior. Advocates of change have to be able to respond to the straightforward question: "Yes, it all sounds good, but what do I do that is different?"

Third, police are wary, a phenomenon that has also been called a "well-planned layback" (Bayley & Bittner, 1984). Experienced officers use a great deal of caution in approaching uncertain situations. They know that people are unpredictable, and that the countless, ordinary, unpredictable police-citizen encounters sometimes mask a genuinely dangerous situation. So they have to learn to see what is not there, to recognize the hidden danger in what is seemingly safe. So their common sense is indeed "uncommon," the ability to see what is not there. Organizational change cannot interfere with an officer's fundamental ability to respond to potential danger, or it will indeed run into a stone wall of cultural resistance.

Fourth, police common sense is rooted in personal experience. One learns police work by doing it and in applying that sensibility to future circumstances. Their ability to control human behavior comes only with experience in dealing with people. Experience is the starch in their cultural tool kit. They will bitterly resist anything that violates their own sense of experience—it is hard-won, it is gained from an appreciation of the real world. Reform, to succeed, must play to street cops' personal experiences. Otherwise it will be rejected out of hand as fantasy, unrealistic, or at worst, liberal academic gibberish.

Fifth, police common sense is about how to coerce people to do things they do not want to do. Citizens, for example, do not like to be arrested. They do not like to be stopped for traffic tickets, to be ordered to do something, or searched. Some people do not like talking to the police at all. Consequently, street cops develop a wide repertoire of skills to coerce people to do all these things. In their grab bag of common lore, the skills and techniques to get citizens to do things rank high.

Reformers cannot simple-mindedly approach cops' coercive skills as something that has to be controlled. This is what the police professionalism movement sought unsuccessfully to do for more than 50 years, and it came to a screeching halt in the 1960s after a series of catastrophic failures showed that it could not be done. If community policing approaches reform from the point of view of trying to control decisions made in the ordinary course of work, it will be doomed to the same inevitable failure.

All of the aspects of common sense listed above—practicality, pragmatism, wariness, personal experience, and a talent for coercion—are at the core of how veteran cops think about their work. These aspects cannot be removed from police culture, and reformers and administrators cannot do an end-run around them. Reform that fails to account for cop common sense will fail utterly. It is the experienced, rough-hewn, and occasionally abrasive street cop who must be incorporated into planned change, who must be its vanguard. As difficult as it may be, this is where successful change has to start.

Old-Fashioned Police Work Is Not Community Policing

One myth of rural community policing is widely held. It is that small-town, rural policing, what some individuals call "old-fashioned policing," is what today we call community policing in urban areas. It is not. This misperception has stemmed from confusion about late-twentieth-century crime and about the nature and purposes of community policing.

The nostalgic image of the nineteenth-century police officer is that of a guardian who acted as a moral binding for small-town nineteenth-century communities. This image fails to recognize the kind of problems confronting the police today. Our problems are greater than controlling unruly teenagers and keeping tabs on who is not going to church on Sunday. As Weisheit and Hawkins have observed (see Chapter 3), the sorts of dilemmas confronting citizens in small towns and rural areas today are sharply different than in times past. Levels of rural crime are increasing, and a traditional homespun response is inadequate. Small communities are becoming centers for the manufacture and distribution of drugs. Distributors of a wide variety of contraband use less-traveled rural byways in the hopes of passing unobserved.

Today we find that spouse and child abuse in rural areas have reached levels similar to urban areas. There is a heightened mistrust of the government in many rural areas today. Across the United States, we see bold and violent paramilitary groups that are outspokenly antigovernment. Poaching has been criminalized, but poachers are widely active. Environmental laws have criminalized a wide variety of farming and ranching practices in many areas, and many traditional ranchers are openly defiant of local crime control. Scenic rural communities are witnessing dramatic increases in population and in levels of crime as urban dwellers seek attractive lifestyle opportunities. Nineteenth-century police myths may be heartwarming, but they offer scant consolation to a small-town cop who is seeing increased immigration of wealthy retirees and is dealing with the threat of escalating drug and gang activity.

How can community-based reform efforts help cops deal with these rural problems? They can contribute in two ways: (1) increasing effectiveness of police to do something about crime through the expansion of line officer skills and knowledge, and (2) decentralization of organizational authority so that officers have more authority to act on their own.

Increasing Effectiveness

Investments in training should focus on making the best of traditional police officer skills. Rural and small-town police today need twentieth-century skills, intelligence, and administrative support. Rural communities need their experience and knowledge more than ever, and we need to add to the mix the resources of the agency to deal with problems they encounter. Resources need to be in the form of training and intelligence particularly designed to assist rural issues.

Peace Officer Standards and Training (POST) has to take a lead in the development of community policing for rural and small-town police. In-service POST training can provide knowledge in the use of computer technologies that are essential to information collection today. POST agencies can assist through expanded classes on community police tactics and on victimization, which will allow cops to focus on the problems that crime causes rather than the current emphasis on the problem makers.

Virtually all states today have Statistical Analysis Centers (SACs), and they need to begin to live up to their promise as centers for the repository of useful information rather than their tendency today to be used to fill the coffers of their home agencies through grant solicitations and indirect funding of positions. SACs can provide agencies with current and ongoing knowledge about types and patterns of regional crime problems. They can identify overlapping problems suitable for joint sheriff-municipal department task forces. SACs hold the greatest potential to coordinate intelligence and gather information for typically underfunded small-town and rural agencies.

Local agencies have tended to support community-type police operations. Various observers of the police have seen how rural police frequently meet with citizens, organize watches and other activities, become involved with schools, and otherwise provide a wide variety of services that are characteristic of community policing activities in more urban communities. These are popular because they are relatively inexpensive. They are also easier to develop in smaller communities, where local police are more likely to be closely tied to their communities than in more urban settings. Volunteers are a necessary resource in sprawling counties, where patrol officers may have to cover 200-300 square miles in a shift. Officers need to be given time and resources to help citizens organize and develop tactics to address their particular problems.

Overcoming Administration

Administrators are quick to blame street cops when directives fail to give satisfactory results, or when they have oversold a reform that was a bad idea. It is not, however, cop culture that needs to be "overcome." There is an accountability problem in American police departments, but it is an administrative problem. Management, as much as anything else, is responsible for the development and sustenance of the darker and more secretive aspects of police culture.

One of the goals of community policing is to expand the discretion street cops have so they can more effectively deal with public order problems. Put academically, this means that the contemporary overemphasis on law enforcement is reconsidered, and a new mandate is proposed that focuses equally on the three pillars of police work—law enforcement, order maintenance, and service. This means that street cops will have more responsibilities. Department brass will have to resist holding street cops more accountable for the mistakes they will make doing community policing or they can expect more CYA.

If street cops are to be more responsible for order maintenance and service activities, how will managers hold them accountable? Put another way, if cops are going to do more (that is, order maintenance and service), are they going to be held responsible for what they will be doing? How and by whom? If managers use the same tired accountability strategies of the past to make officers responsible for their activities, community policing will never make it as viable reform. It will be no more than a set of circumlocutions, as Klockars (1991) so eloquently put it, for obscuring the coercive nature of real police work. Managers have to take a different tack—they have to learn to let go a little (or a lot, in some cases).

Chief John Turner of Mountlake Terrace, Washington, is an eloquent advocate of administrative innovation for community policing. He exhorts administrators to learn how to relax their grip on line behavior, to cease trying to control everything that line officers do. His is a forceful view, and it is a vision central to the theme of this chapter. If street cops are to be advocates for change, they have to be trusted. It is not enough to speak lofty platitudes about their contribution to local communities. Management has to learn to trust their rank and file. They have to accept and live with mistakes, knowing that mistakes go with the territory.

Administrators face a dilemma—on the one hand, they want to employ community policing strategies and reap the positive press that tends to accompany such ventures. On the other hand, they want to hold officers accountable to be sure that they are doing community policing and that they do not "screw up" in the process. This latter goal, accountability, can stifle innovation. Rather than facilitating community policing, it can encourage the most hostile aspects of the police culture and close the door on all efforts to create a viable community policing program.

Conclusion

The key to successful community policing cannot be found in an administrative directive. It lies in the skills and wisdom of experienced street cops. Community policing will work to the extent that it is congruent with their daily activities. It will fail when it obstructs their moral commitment to their assigned beat and their practical, commonsense way of solving problems they encounter in their work.

A cop's work is a beat, a dominion over territory, property, and people. The foundations of culture are the tool kit of tactics and strategies for dealing with that responsibility. When those ways of doing things become a part of the organization's traditions and are accepted as the right way to do things, an organizational culture is in full flower. It is carried primarily by mature, seasoned officers. Successful change will occur among them or it will not occur. It is time we moved beyond the naive notion that police culture must somehow be wiped out, and instead learn to appreciate it for what it is, a celebration of a way of life that seeks to sort out good and bad in its commonsense way of thinking about them, as all cultures do.

To change the police organization, Ahern (1972) once observed, you have to change the hearts and minds of its patrol officers. This is certainly true for community policing today. The key to successful community policing lies in the way that administrators engage a street cop's heart. The rank and file need to be involved in some capacity in all planning sessions, in the development of training programs, and in the ongoing evaluation of their work. They must be given self-accountability.

Administrators should make efforts to provide resources for officers to deal with problems that are encountered. To paraphrase Skolnick and Bayley (1986), administrators should genuinely consider the ideas and suggestions that street cops have about their work. They will often be practical, mundane, and they may seem inconsequential. Yet this is the nature of their work, and it is common to the types of problems they encounter. And administrators must go beyond this. They need to abandon the punitive accountability strategies that have undermined street-management relations and bring an air of openness and support to the rank and file. When they do so, the "Jack Wilsons" who strengthen police work everywhere can become agents of the future as well as carriers of department and community traditions.

References

Ahern, J. (1972). *Police in Trouble: Our Frightening Crisis in Law* Enforcement. New York, NY: Hawthorn Books.

Bayley, D., and E. Bittner (1984). "Learning the Skills in Policing." *Law and Contemporary Problems* 47:35-39.

Klockars, C.B. (1991). "The Rhetoric of Community Policing." In C. Klockars and S. Mastrofski (eds.), *Thinking about Policing*, Second Edition. New York, NY: McGraw-Hill, Inc.

Manning, P. (1977). *Police Work: The Social Organization of Policing*. Cambridge, MA: The MIT Press.

Skolnick, J., and D. Bayley (1986). *The New Blue Line: Police Innovation in Six American Cities*. New York, NY: The Free Press.

Wilson, J.Q. (1968). *Varieties of Police Behavior: The Management of Law and Order in Eight Communities*. Cambridge, MA: Harvard University Press.

Getting to Know Your Employees Better   8

Edmund F. McGarrell
Michigan State University

Rosanne London
Eastern Washington University

Socorro Benitez
Eastern Washington University

Introduction

The community policing movement, given the emphasis on building partnerships with the community, naturally entails an outward focus for the law enforcement agency. Perhaps less obvious is the immediate need to examine the internal organization. If the organization is to transform itself and successfully create community partnerships, the structure, culture, values, and goals of the organization must be aligned with the community policing philosophy. For the chief or sheriff, this means that there must be an understanding of the organization itself. In this chapter, we review the use of two strategies for gaining a deeper understanding of the organization: the employee survey and focus group interviews with organizational members.

Background

Since the early 1990s, the Washington State Institute for Community Oriented Policing (WSICOP) has worked with a number of law enforcement agencies interested in implementing a community policing philosophy. As an initial step in changing the organization, many of these agencies decided to undertake employee and citizen surveys (see Chapter 12 for a discussion of citizen surveys) and to conduct focus group interviews. In this chapter, we illustrate the value of employee surveys by presenting illustrative findings from four agencies. Spokane Police Department serves an eastern Washington city of approximately 180,000 urban residents (McGarrell & Thurman, 1994). The department employs approximately 400 commissioned and noncommissioned employees. The Spokane County Sheriff's Office (WA) serves the surrounding county, which is a mix of urban, small-town, and rural areas with a population of approximately 190,000

(Erp, Lovrich & Briney, 1995b). The sheriff's office employs approximately 440 employees. The Moses Lake Police Department serves a small town of approximately 11,000 people in central Washington (see Erp, Lovrich & Briney, 1995a). The department has 48 employees. The Ellensburg Police Department serves a city of 12,000 and has 26 employees. The focus group interviews conducted with employee groups were conducted in one of the above agencies.

Key Issues and Discussion

The Goals of Employee Surveys

At a general level, the goal of the employee survey is to allow the organization embarking on major organizational change to "establish a means by which it can assess the degree to which that change results in both intended improvements and unanticipated undesirable consequences" (Erp, Lovrich & Briney, 1995a:2). More specifically, there are at least three reasons to conduct employee surveys as the agency adopts community policing:

- Provide a means of assessing the organization
- Pinpoint potential problem areas
- Benchmark organizational change

One of the lessons of organizational change is that it takes a long time. One consequence is that employees often grow frustrated with the slow pace of change and, in turn, grow cynical that anything "new" is really occurring. Law enforcement managers are likely to hear "nothing has changed around here" and "this too shall pass" when pronouncements about the implementation of community policing do not immediately result in organizational transformation. Having hard data from a survey or, better yet, a series of surveys can effectively counteract these cynics if the data show how the organization is changing.

Conducting the Employee Survey

Rare is the police executive with either the experience or the time to conduct a formal survey of the agency's employees. For this reason, a number of law enforcement agencies have found it useful to work with local colleges and universities to conduct the survey. When doing so, it is important that employees throughout the organization be involved in the planning and administration of the survey. The survey can be part of an effort to "announce" that things are going to change. Part of that change, if community policing is to be effectively implemented, is that employees from all ranks will be involved in organizational decisionmaking—including the survey itself. One approach that has been successful in the agencies that WSICOP has worked with is to create a vertical team (meaning it includes employees from all units and ranks) to plan and implement the survey. The team can then work with the researchers to conduct the survey. In this way, it is "our" survey as opposed to a project of outsiders.

Care must be given to ensure anonymity and to answer questions employees will have about why the survey is being conducted. The vertical team is often in the best position to answer such questions. In the small agency, it may be necessary to exclude questions on some demographics and positions within the agency because they could create fear of being identified (e.g., in one agency, the only female supervisor expressed concern that her responses could be readily identified).

Topics

The surveys conducted by WSICOP (a sample employee survey appears in Appendix A), though altered to meet needs of the specific organization, generally tap into the following dimensions about the organization:

- Job Diagnosis (Motivation, Satisfaction, Stress)
- Understanding of and Attitudes toward Community Policing
- Work-Related Problems
- Perception of Neighborhood Problems

In the following sections, we provide examples of findings from our surveys that illustrate the utility of gathering information on these dimensions.

Job Diagnosis. As previous chapters have noted, the successful implementation of community policing entails considerable organizational change. To support this transition, the employee survey can provide information on the current "health" of the organization and on the success of efforts to change the organization over time.

Organizational research has identified several dimensions of work that relate to levels of motivation and satisfaction among workers. Key among these are the meaningfulness of the work (the individual perceives the work as worthwhile and important), the responsibility of the job (the individual must feel personally accountable for the outcomes of the work), and the extent to which the worker has knowledge of the results of his or her efforts (Hackman & Oldham, 1980). To the extent that these qualities are present, the employees are likely to be highly motivated, to perform high-quality work, to be satisfied, and to have lower rates of absenteeism and turnover.

Sections 3-5 of the WSICOP survey (see Appendix A) include standardized items that measure job motivation and job satisfaction. Because the items are standardized, the organization can compare itself to other law enforcement agencies and other types of organizations. If the surveys are repeated, the question of whether community policing is producing more satisfied and motivated workers can be answered.

In the surveys conducted by WSICOP, law enforcement agencies tend to score high on the meaningfulness of the work but low on task identity ("the degree to which the job requires completion of a 'whole' and identifiable piece of work" (Hackman & Oldham, 1980:78) and the feedback dimension. This likely reflects the case-processing nature of the reactive police agency. Calls come in, a response is made, and the case is passed on. In contrast, the problem-solving community policing agency offers the promise of allowing officers to address a broader problem and, if successful, to see the fruits of the effort. Although it is too early in the community policing movement and adequate data are not yet available, initial results from the Spokane Police Department are suggestive. The first employee survey, conducted in 1992 when the organization was in the earliest stages of community policing, showed that it scored slightly higher than a comparable agency that had not reached the same stage in the adoption of community policing. Eighteen months later, although the changes were slight, the Spokane Police Department had increased its scores on job motivation and job satisfaction (McGarrell & Thurman, 1994).

A similar finding that emerged was that employees within the police department who expressed a positive orientation toward community policing had higher levels of job motivation and job satisfaction, lower levels of stress, and expressed a greater attachment to the organization (McGarrell & Thurman, 1994). That is, within an organization clearly committed to community policing, employees whose values and philosophy are most congruent with the organizational philosophy appear to be the most satisfied, motivated, and committed.

The employee survey can also be used for more fine-tuned analyses within the organization. In Moses Lake, the survey revealed that female employees within the organization were less satisfied with their work than were males (Erp, Lovrich & Briney, 1995a). This knowledge can then be used to assess whether these problems are specific to roles or whether there are matters of concern with the organizational climate. In another example, the Spokane Police Department survey showed that the records unit scored particularly low on job motivation and satisfaction and very high on stress. Further investigation revealed that employees within the unit felt they were merely passing on paper without any idea of how their work affected others (i.e., lack of feedback). Given this analysis, the supervisor of the unit was able to craft responses to these problems (see subsequent discussion of customer surveys).

It is important to note that the surveys allow the organization to assess how it currently stands in meeting the needs of its employees. Surveys can help pinpoint specific areas of concern within the organization and, if the survey is repeated, develop concrete data on whether the organization is changing in a positive direction.

Understanding of and Attitudes Toward Community Policing. Sections 6 and 7 of the survey instrument include a number of items that tap into perceptions of the police role, attitudes toward citizens and police-community relations, and problems related to implementing community policing. Although not used in all the surveys, these items allow us to create an index of community policing orientation. In the Spokane Police Department, this index provided useful information that indicated older officers were as committed to the new philosophy as were younger officers. The survey also indicated that the biggest problem officers perceived was in striking a balance between long-standing responsibilities (e.g., calls for service) and the added duties brought on by the community policing role (something identified in Chapter 4 as a serious concern on the part of police chiefs).

These items also can provide a benchmark of organizational progress. Again, using the Spokane Police Department as an example (the only department in which the WSICOP survey has been repeated to date), the second survey indicated that there was much less confusion about the community policing role and that lack of training was less an obstacle than had been the case in the initial survey. Thus, whereas the initial survey demonstrated the need for training, the second survey indicated that the training had been successfully delivered.

Work-Related Problems and Perception of Neighborhood Problems. Sections 2 and 8-10 of the WSICOP survey ask employees to assess both internal organizational problems and external community problems. One of the interesting patterns that was observed in Washington was that in the Spokane Police Department, the overwhelming problems were considered to be an inadequate budget that produced inadequate staffing and excessive workload. In contrast, in the smaller Ellensburg Police Department, excessive workload was not considered as serious a problem. Were this pattern to be observed generally, it would suggest that one advantage small agencies may have in implementing community policing is that they are not overwhelmed by continual calls for service.

The section on neighborhood problems is particularly useful if combined with similar responses from citizens. For example, in Ellensburg, the police highlighted traditional crime problems (e.g., burglary and illegal drugs) as the most significant problems, whereas citizens were most concerned with traffic, parking, and downtown loitering by youths. This information was very useful to the department as it attempted to work with the citizens on resolving local problems.

The Customer Survey

Chief David Couper from the Madison, Wisconsin, Police Department gained attention when he began to conduct a short customer survey with citizens who had contact with the police (Mastrofski & Wadman, 1991). This one-page survey, which focuses on perceived professionalism, helpfulness, courtesy, and similar attributes, also has been used in Spokane by the records unit. Following the general survey, which indicated low satisfaction and motivation within the unit, the supervisor decided to conduct a customer survey as a way of providing feedback to the unit. The survey revealed that both internal and external customers were very appreciative of the unit's work. The information came as a surprise to employees of the unit and served to boost morale. The point is that valuable information can be gleaned from short, specialized surveys as well as the more major undertaking of the general employee survey discussed above.

Focus Group Interviews as an Additional Source of Information

The focus group is "an interview style designed for small groups" that involves "discussions addressing a particular topic of interest or relevance to the group and the researcher" (Berg, 1995; see also Stewart & Shamdasani, 1991). One of the main advantages of focus groups is the amount and, particularly, depth of information they provide. In contrast to the survey in which respondents are limited to predetermined responses (checking a box), focus group participants are able to give opinions and explain meanings. This format also allows the facilitator to probe for further understanding and to move to issues that arise during the focus group discussion that may not have been envisioned prior to the session.

Law enforcement agencies may choose to employ focus groups prior to the construction of a survey, as a follow-up to a survey, or as an alternative to conducting a survey of the entire organization. As a precursor to a formal survey, the focus group may suggest topics that need to be studied systematically through a survey. For example, focus groups may indicate that employees are confused about the new role expectations associated with the community policing philosophy. A follow-up survey could then indicate whether the confusion is widespread throughout the organization or whether it tends to be confined to particular shifts or units. Similarly, the survey could be used to pinpoint the nature of the confusion.

Focus groups can be particularly valuable as a follow-up to the formal employee survey. For example, the survey might indicate that the most frequently mentioned obstacle to community policing is mid-level supervisors. It is unlikely, however, that the survey will uncover the nature of the problem with mid-level supervision. Are they philosophically opposed to community policing? Is it their adherence to outdated policies and procedures? Is it a matter of lack of communication throughout all levels of the organization? The focus group offers the opportunity to probe deeply into issues identified in the survey.

A third use of the focus group is as a source of information about the organization, or particular units within the agency, when a full survey is impractical. With adequate consideration given to issues of participant selection, the focus group can be a valuable tool for organizational assessment.

Using Focus Group Interviews in a Law Enforcement Agency. Forethought and planning are required to get the most from focus group sessions. The questions must be designed to tap into issues of interest and to foster dialogue. It is important to keep in mind that the focus group interview is intended to gather information. Consequently, selection of participants for a particular session must be done in a way that will enhance, not discourage, open dialogue. For example, for some purposes it may not be wise to include supervisors and their employees in the same focus group, because the presence of supervisors might preclude frank and open discussion.

The size of the organization will dictate the number of focus groups to be conducted. Generally, focus groups should include anywhere from six to ten participants. For larger agencies, it may be unrealistic to have all employees participate in focus groups. In this instance, sampling can be used to select participants. Employees can be grouped into units, shifts, roles, or other meaningful categories, and then focus group participants can be randomly sampled from these groupings. In creating these groupings, it is important that all segments of the organization be included. The random selection process ensures that the widest variety of voices within the organization are heard. In smaller departments, it may be possible to include all members of the organization in a single focus group session. This has the added benefit of expressing to employees that management cares about their opinions and suggestions.

Scheduling can be complicated in a law enforcement agency due to shift schedules and the need for 24-hour coverage of many functions. Additionally, it is important that the focus group interviews occur in relative temporal proximity. Employees will talk to one another, and long lapses between sessions can mean that later groups have been influenced by members of earlier sessions (or other events occurring in the department or community).

Beyond the participants themselves, the key players in the focus group project are the overall coordinator, facilitator, and recorder. The coordinator is responsible for overseeing all steps in planning and implementing the project. The facilitator acts as the moderator of the focus group session. The facilitator must explain the purpose of the project and establish rapport with participants. The facilitator must keep the group focused on the issues at hand, enlist the participation of all group members, and moderate any heated discussions that may arise. The recorder attempts to write down all comments being made by group members. The typical focus group session lasts approximately one hour.

Examples of Focus Group Findings. The value of the focus group is the depth and richness of the data that can be generated. The following examples are drawn from one law enforcement organization from Washington state that conducted focus group interviews as a follow-up to an organization-wide employee survey.

An employee survey had indicated that employees were clear that management wanted to move toward community policing and that most employees had some understanding of the community policing philosophy. The survey also revealed, however, that some employees were resistant to this organizational transition. What was unclear were the factors that were producing this resistance. The focus group interviews (see Appendix B for an example of a focus group employee interview schedule) indicated that while most employees believed community policing was good in theory, they felt it was unrealistic to implement it with existing organizational resources. Other employees reported that only a small portion of the department's employees actually had the opportunity to engage in community policing activities. Particularly among patrol officers, most felt they were too busy responding to calls for service to really have the time to engage in community policing. The focus group sessions also suggested that the department needed to give more attention to explaining the community policing philosophy externally and to engage citizens, elected officials, and other public agencies in the "partnership" component of community policing.

These were all concerns that either had not been uncovered or were only hinted at in the employee survey. The focus group sessions proved valuable in bringing about a more complete understanding of attitudes, perceptions, values, and emotions present among organization members.

Conclusion

The outward focus of the community policing movement should not blind the law enforcement executive to the internal processes that will, in large measure, determine the success of the implementation of community policing. The employee survey and focus group interview are important tools in the arsenal of the chief or sheriff seeking to change the organization for the benefit of all employees.

References

Berg, B.L. (1995). *Qualitative Research Methods for the Social Sciences*, Second Edition. Boston, MA: Allyn and Bacon.

Erp, M.J., N.P. Lovrich, and J. Briney (1995a). *Moses Lake Police Department: Baseline Assessment Survey Results, 1995*. Spokane, WA: Washington State Institute for Community Oriented Policing.

_____ (1995b). *Spokane County Sheriff's Office: Baseline Assessment Survey Results, 1995.* Spokane, WA: Washington State Institute for Community Oriented Policing.

Hackman, J.R., and G.R. Oldham (1980). *Work Redesign.* Reading, MA: Addison-Wesley.

Mastrofski, S.D., and R.C. Wadman (1991). "Personnel and Agency Performance Measurement." In W.A. Geller (ed.), *Local Government Police Management.* Washington, DC: International City Management Association.

McGarrell, E.F., and Q.C. Thurman (1994). *Findings from the 1993 Spokane Police Department Employee Survey: Final Report.* Spokane, WA: Washington State Institute for Community Oriented Policing.

Stewart, D., and P. Shamdasani (1991). *Focus Groups: Theory and Practice.* Newbury Park, CA: Sage Publications.

Linking the Right Person to the Right Job: Selecting, Training, and Retaining Officers to Do Community Policing

9

Ricky S. Gutierrez
California State University-Sacramento

Quint C. Thurman
Southwest Texas State University

Introduction

Change from a traditional model to a community policing model requires sheriffs and police chiefs to rethink how they conduct many aspects of police business. One of the most important is the issue of selecting and then appropriately training the "right people" to do community policing. While it is not necessarily the case that the usual motives (e.g., altruism, interest in working out-of-doors, etc.) that have attracted people to law enforcement careers in the past will differ from those of the people who might be drawn to community policing, it may well be that community policing does require higher skill levels in some key areas than in others. In particular, this chapter suggests that chiefs and sheriffs might consider ways to include their communities in selecting, training, and retaining officers to do community policing.

Key Issues

During the past 50 years, police officers have been recruited for their good physical condition, their interest in crime control, and their ability to follow command decisions without hesitation. This explains why agencies often hired former military personnel as patrol officers. What is not known is how well these attributes fit contemporary policing duties or whether these qualities were sufficient by themselves to help officers do a good job.

Observations of police personnel on the job suggest that there is much more to it than might first be suspected.

While a traditional focus on law enforcement might have been appropriate in an age of police reform and professionalization (and even during emergency response situations in present-day police organizations), it seems that such an orientation is not all that is required to carry out community policing. After all, community policing emphasizes a broader crime-control mission that relies on the development of a more participative style of management—one that emphasizes good communication skills to encourage citizens to become involved in crime prevention and problem solving. Talking "with" citizens rather than talking "to" them is a big part of doing community policing well.

Studies of small cities and rural counties across the United States indicate that local residents overwhelmingly support community policing practices. In fact, citizen surveys suggest that communities are eager to welcome community policing if only their police forces would let them know how citizens might help. Similarly, McEwen (1995) found that community policing is heavily supported by law enforcement professionals. His results from a national study indicated that more than 80 percent of the police chiefs surveyed had either begun implementation of community policing or were planning to do so in the near future. The challenge for law enforcement agencies is to prepare themselves to live up to both the public's and the profession's expectations.

The goal of this chapter is to examine three important components of personnel management—selection, training, and retention. The goals of community policing are changing job descriptions and those who hire new personnel must consider which qualities best fit the mold of a community policing officer. At the same time, supervisors must decide how best to motivate new officers and veterans alike to perform community policing duties. Similarly, law enforcement executives must increase their awareness of community policing performance issues if they are to send clear messages to supervisory personnel about how best to assess the value of community policing in an organization.

Selection

Rural agencies today seem poised to reexamine performance expectations as sheriff's deputies and police officers become agents of social change. Questions about how their attitudes, values, and beliefs might change as organizational philosophies move from a professional model of policing to a community orientation must be decided by each organization. In many ways the inner character of those drawn to policing will not differ. For example, Storms, Penn, and Tenzell's (1990:43) study of three police agencies suggested that "both traditional and non-traditional police officers rate police personnel as warm, emotional, and flexible." What is more apt to require change is how officers project themselves to the public. Consider the following about police versus citizen expectations from a recent community policing text:

Gerald Heuett, Jr., a Phoenix police officer and a technical advisor to the Arizona Regional Community Policing Institute, when training police about what citizens expect of them, uses an exercise that helps distinguish a professional police perspective from one that views community policing as its primary goal. He begins the exercise by asking a class of 30 or so [police officers] to identify the characteristics of the ideal patrol officer. Typically they describe a person who has courage, is brave under fire, and who can be counted on to come to the aid of a fellow officer in trouble. Heuett next asks them to describe the officer who they might want on the scene of a hypothetical situation involving their own son or daughter in a serious automobile crash. Here the group describes an [ideal] officer in terms such as compassionate, sensitive, fair, and calm under pressure. This exercise puts police in the same position as the citizens they serve. Heuett believes that the striking difference in the responses to the first and second questions is that in the second the participants have unknowingly answered the same way that citizens do when they are asked to describe their image of the ideal police officer. Although police admire colleagues who exhibit bravery and know how to take charge in dangerous situations, when the people they care most about are the recipients of police services, they prefer to be treated with compassion and fairness just as ordinary citizens do (Thurman et al., 2001:168).

Developing a more relaxed posture when working with the public in non-emergency situations also might require officers to make a similar adjustment in working relationships with other officers. Veteran officers who can show leadership by demonstrating compassion and concern for the citizens they serve can do much to improve the subculture of policing that might resist the idea that arrest is the only tool the agency can use to preserve order. Similarly, veteran leadership in favor of community policing will help set the tone for new recruits. As noted by former Minneapolis police chief Anthony Bouza (1990:71), many officers who run afoul of an organization and the public it serves start out as highly qualified recruits who are socialized into a "secret society where a code of loyalty, silence, secretiveness, and isolation reigns."

In theory, police officers and sheriff's deputies should be recruited for: (1) their ability to remain composed in stressful situations, (2) interactive skills, (3) commitment to community partnerships, and (4) service orientation. The ability to "keep your head about you when all others are losing theirs" will remain as an important trait in hiring competent policing professionals. What really is new is the recognition that good verbal communication skills are crucial in the age of community policing. Talking with citizens about crime problems requires the same ability that talking with crime victims and witnesses has had in the past, when organizations only wanted to "get the facts" about a crime. And "jawboning" has always been a good way to talk with criminal suspects or informants to learn about criminal activity. What differs here is learning to talk and listen on an equal footing with a wider representation of people than police officers have been used to previously.

It will be up to law enforcement executives to work with their managers and veteran officers to identify the qualities they think will best serve their organization and the local citizens with whom they will interact as they join police-community partnerships. Chiefs and sheriffs will have to consider how verbal is verbal enough, how much value they place on individual officers being able to think on their feet, and specific qualities that their communities might value in particular. Having thought these things through, the next step should be to develop adequate means to screen for desirable candidates.

Screening

The primary means used by many large police agencies to screen candidates comes from the Minnesota Multiphasic Personality Inventory (MMPI). This instrument is mainly used to predict aggression, ambivalence, deception, depression, hysteria, or other forms of psychopathology prior to hiring an applicant as a police officer (Hargrave, Hiatt, Ogard & Karr, 1994). Another technique used to predict police officer performance is the Inwald Personality Inventory or IPI (Inwald, Knatz & Shusman, 1983). The IPI was developed in order to correct for flaws exposed in research that targeted the validity of the MMPI as the sole psychological test used to screen police officer candidates (see Shusman et al., 1987).

Test items may focus on almost any aspect of intellectual or emotional functioning, including personality traits, attitudes, intelligence, or emotional concerns. Tests usually are administered by a qualified clinical or industrial psychologist, according to professional and ethical principles. Interpretation is based on a comparison of the individual's responses with those previously obtained to establish appropriate standards for test scores. However, the usefulness of any psychological test depends on its accuracy in predicting behavior. By providing information about the likelihood of a person's response to a particular situation, tests aid in making a variety of decisions. They are used in industrial and organizational settings for selection and classification. Selection procedures provide guidelines for accepting or rejecting candidates for jobs. Classification procedures, which are more complex, try to identify the types of positions for which an individual is best suited.

Most of the criticisms of various tests come from the overvaluation of and inappropriate reliance on test results in making major life decisions (e.g., hiring, promotion, and firing). Some technical flaws exist in all tests. Because of this, it is important for police administrators to use a wide range of information that might be relevant to the selection process. Typically, psychologists agree that using tests to screen potential job applicants can pose problems without carefully considering past and present resources or motivation. For example, because many tests tend to draw on skills associated with white, middle-class values and functioning, they may discriminate against blue-collar workers and minority groups. As long as differences in education, cultural norms, values, and personal experiences exist, test results will continue to be biased against certain applicants.

As noted above, agencies are challenged to think through the values that they wish successful employees to have. Pencil-and-paper tests cannot guarantee successful screening, as large departments have discovered. In 1990, the International Association of Chiefs of Police supported the use of multiple screening tools to improve hiring practices. While agencies commonly use several approaches to rate applicants, including background investigations, interviews, applications, civil service tests, agility tests, and psychological assessments, "to be of any value, a predictor must be able to predict future performance on the job with some demonstrable level of accuracy" (Dwyer & Prien, 1990:177).

When psychological testing is a major component in the screening process, it supposedly is the case that the test chosen is helpful in predicting some aspect of an applicant's personality that may impair his or her performance as a police officer in the future. Obviously, eliminating potential bad apples is a major concern for police agencies in light of recent national coverage of police misconduct and the threat of civil lawsuits. However, a focus on overly narrow attributes that have historically been linked to success in the field may restrict chiefs and sheriffs from choosing applicants with other qualities, who seem well-suited to community policing. As a result, it may be the case that police organizations are hiring people based on out-of-date standards that are not suited to deliver problem-oriented and community-oriented policing. However, the criteria for choosing officers based on ideal community policing skills have not been well established as of yet.

Inwald (1988) recognizes 12 caveats for sheriffs and chiefs when choosing tests for screening applicants using simple pencil-and-paper tests. Police agencies should be critical of:

- Tests with little or no supporting validation research.

- Tests that claim they only replace the "polygraph."

- Studies that are not based on the prediction model of validation.

- Studies that do not inform readers how many people were incorrectly predicted to have job problems.

- Tests that claim to predict dangerous or violent behavior.

- Studies that report significant correlations as evidence of their validity.

- Studies that use small numbers of people to predict important job performance outcomes.

- Studies that have not been cross-validated.

- Claims that tests are valid for use with occupational groups for which validation studies have not yet been conducted.

- Studies based on test questionnaires or tests filled out anonymously.

- Studies that have not used real job candidates as subjects in their validation efforts.

- Tests whose validation studies have been designed, conducted, and published only by the test developer or publishing company without replication by other totally independent psychologists or agencies.

As early as 1981, Goleman urged human resource managers to connect job analysis (e.g., what traits do exemplary community police officers possess?) with predictive testing by changing the criteria by which applicants are hired. Rather than simply relying on a well-rounded personality profile, a comprehensive battery of situation-based simulations could be used to assess how well one will perform before he or she is hired. The Assessment Center (Pynes & Bernardin, 1992) is an approach that parallels Goleman's situationally based tests.

Assessment centers that focus on different skills by using job analysis as a basis for designing a variety of scenarios common to everyday police work are used to supplement traditional pencil and paper testing and are routinely used for hiring police chiefs and public safety directors. According to Pynes and Bernardin (1992:43), "the variety of exercises used in an assessment center allows raters to base their decisions on multiple sources of data, thereby reducing measurement errors." Mini-assessment centers could be used to screen top patrol officer applicants too, with the added twist being to bring citizens into the process as judges. This would accomplish two important goals. First, valuable citizen input would add a wider perspective to the agency's viewpoint. Second, bringing citizens in clearly underscores the importance of civilians in a police-community partnership.

Training and Performance Assessment

As job descriptions move from reactive styles of policing to proactive and coactive styles, issues that relate to community policing training and performance become more important. While policies and procedures are critically important for limiting officer discretion in emergency situations, officers engaging in community policing will be expected to exercise greater discretion in a wider variety of daily activities. Making good decisions that benefit both the agency and the community will depend heavily on training.

Community policing invites increased contact between law-abiding citizens and police. Because of this, training officers in interpersonal interaction, ethnic diversity, drug and alcohol awareness, and domestic violence issues cannot be ignored. Effective problem solving will require a greater understanding of the best ways to handle sensitive situations among both patrol officers and those who supervise them. Curricula in community colleges and universities have begun to adapt their criminal justice course offerings in ways that better prepare officers for the kinds of problems they will see in the field.

Another resource for community policing training is the peer assessment approach. Peer assessment can be used to gain insight into how well police officers function. Schumacher, Scogin, Howland, and McGee (1992:292) found that "peer assessment may be a valuable tool in the prediction of success in the law enforcement field" and "can be used to assist in the selection and screening of applicants." Peer assessments have been used in the past to evaluate officer performance and can be used as an additional training tool. Highly visible areas of performance can be assessed using a panel of outstanding employees who exhibit desirable community policing qualities.

By encouraging departmental unity and officer accountability through fair and equitable performance measures, community mistrust of the police can be replaced over time by mutual respect among all groups who join together to build community resources. After all, community-oriented public safety should be a priority for all law-abiding citizens. Building a better community is an investment that benefits both officers and citizens alike.

Retention

As the skills for potential police applicants move toward the mission and goals of community policing, performance appraisals that encompass input from citizens, supervisors, and peers can be designed to ensure that the police-community partnership remains intact. As currently designed, police performance measures tend to evaluate officers with respect to how many tickets are written, officer response times to calls for service, the ability to follow top-down decisions, and the tidiness of their appearance.

In order to present a total picture of how well officers perform in a more "people-oriented" atmosphere, more attention has to be paid to additional sources of information that might tell us something about community policing skills. For example, the number and quality of police officer-initiated citizen contacts might be important indicators of officer performance. Agencies may have to implement ways for officers to record daily contacts or administer periodic surveys of community members to assess performance. This can be done by random callbacks to people contacted or through systematic surveys of neighborhoods or jurisdictions served by particular officers. Letters of appreciation from satisfied citizens also might be solicited. The task at hand is for police managers, personnel specialists, citizens, test administrators, and union representatives to agree on acceptable standards. In order to accomplish this goal, extensive collaboration will be required of all concerned. Discussions concerning how to (and to what extent) training and performance criteria can be revised in order to reflect an interest in issues relevant to the community are timely.

In a study of supercops, Reming (1988:163) found that perceptions of unevenness in officer production and effectiveness "may be attributed to the difficulty of defining and measuring police productivity, and the lack of consensus as to what constitutes a productive or non-productive police officer." Falkenberg, Gaines, and Cordner (1991:358) add that "police officers should be evaluated on the performance of important tasks, not on the extent to which raters think they may possess

Schumacher, J., F. Scogin, K. Howland, and J. McGee (1992). "The Relation of Peer Assessment to Future Law Enforcement Performance." *Criminal Justice and Behavior* 19:286-293.

Shusman, E., R. Inwald, and H. Knatz (1987). "A Cross Validation Study of Police Recruit Performance as Predicted by the IPI and MMPI." *Journal of Police Science and Administration* 15:162-169.

Storms, L.H., N.F. Penn, and J.H. Tenzell (1990). "Policeman's Perception of Real and Ideal Policemen." *Journal of Police Science and Administration* 17:40-43.

Thurman, Q.C., and P. Bogen (1996). "Research Note: Spokane Community Police Officers Revisited." *American Journal of Police* 15:97-116.

Thurman, Q.C., P. Bogen, and A. Giacomazzi (1993). "Program Monitoring and Community Policing: A Process Evaluation of Community Policing Efforts in Spokane, Washington." *American Journal of Police* 12:89-114.

Thurman, Q.C., J. Zhao, and A. Giacomazzi (2001). *Community Policing in a Community Era*. Los Angeles, CA: Roxbury.

Section III
The Community Role in Community Policing

The Police and Community Organizing 10

David E. Duffee
University at Albany

This chapter reviews the concept of community as an interaction network composed of local and nonlocal actors. After identifying three different strategies for changing these interaction patterns, it examines the different roles that the police might play in these change efforts. These change efforts are also known as strategies for "community organizing." While each organizing strategy has drawbacks and strengths, the strategy that has been the most successful in many high-crime neighborhoods may be the most difficult for police officials to adopt or support. Some specific actions within police agencies might reduce their traditional resistance to effective involvement in community change.

Key Issues

What Is a Community?

The most common elements in definitions of community are:

- People (number and characteristics)

- Interaction patterns (among the people and among the organizations they form)

- Shared ties (such as common views, experience, values, problems)

- A specific locality (the place in which the people live, interact, etc.).

The term "community" is sometimes used to refer to groups of people who do not share a common place, such as a community of common interests. "Community" is also used to connote places where the residents interact only in specific ways, usually implying "tightly knit" and "supportive" interactions. But these uses of the term are not helpful in thinking about communities and policing. First, place-based communities are still relevant because police serve people in legal and physical space. Second, all place-based communities in a jurisdiction must be served, not just those that are tightly knit or highly cooperative. Thus, for purposes of this essay, community refers to the nature of a people and the nature of what they share and how they interact in a specific locality (Lyon, 1987).

How big a locality? The issue of community size, or locating community boundaries, is perhaps the most difficult aspect of community on a conceptual level. But as a practical matter, as in policing, conducting research, or organizing, the size problem appears manageable. The locality most often chosen in practice to distinguish one community from another is the residential neighborhood (Skogan & Maxfield, 1981). This focus on neighborhood, rather than a larger area—such as a collection of neighborhoods and a central business district—can work, as long as we keep in mind that many elements of local government and the local economy are then considered nonlocal forces, although still crucial to life within the neighborhood-community.

The Internal/External Problem

Another important aspect of community is that it is not a self-contained social system. Most of what happens in communities is attributable either to people informally organized into family and friendship networks or formally organized into organizational networks. But neither all the informal nor all the formal interactions important to the community occur only among units in the community. Families, friends, and organizations also interact with other units outside the community space. For example, many of the organizations that operate in a community are parts of larger organizations (e.g., police substations, branches of chain stores, neighborhood schools in a citywide system). They are controlled to a large degree by headquarters or central office officials, distant from any specific community and concerned for many communities at once.

Because communities are not self-contained systems, they are often examined as "interactional fields" in which a variety of local and nonlocal forces meet or connect through interaction networks (Hope, 1995). While it is tempting to talk of nonlocal as "external" and local as "internal," this can be misleading. It is important to remember that forces with nonlocal origin must be viewed as "in," and a vital part of, the local community. For example, high unemployment and high vacancy rates in the small city of Schenectady, New York, once the home of General Electric, are in large part due to international economic change and GE withdrawal from the community (Rabrenovic, 1996). These changes are not "outside" Schenectady but very much as part of what it is today.

Patterns of Local/Nonlocal Interaction

Most research distinguishes four basic patterns of community interaction (see Figure 10.1): those in which local groups are segmented (cells A and C) or unified (cells B and D), and are either influential (cells A and B) or not influential (cells C and D) with nonlocal groups (Hallman, 1984; Langworthy & Travis, 1994; Spergel, 1976; Warren, 1978). This model of interactional fields suggests four broad types of community.

In pluralistic localities (cell A), various local groups (represented by the circles) are fairly influential with nonlocal entities (as depicted by the solid vertical lines), but have relatively weak connections to each other (as depicted by the dashed horizontal lines), so that these groups are segmented, or poorly coordinated. In mobilized localities (cell B), local groups present a unified front to nonlocal actors: internal decisions about what the community needs represent a neighborhood consensus, and collective demands are made upon nonlocal authorities. In controlled localities (cell C), local groups are segmented and none of them have much influence over decisions made by nonlocal groups. In this kind of community there may be little trust or cooperation among neighbors, and local groups may feel powerless to affect nonlocal decisions. In communal localities (cell D), local groups are unified, but local leaders frequently do not participate in nonlocal decisions about the area, and nonlocal resources are usually not sought to supplement local resources.

Figure 10.1
Four Community Interactional Fields

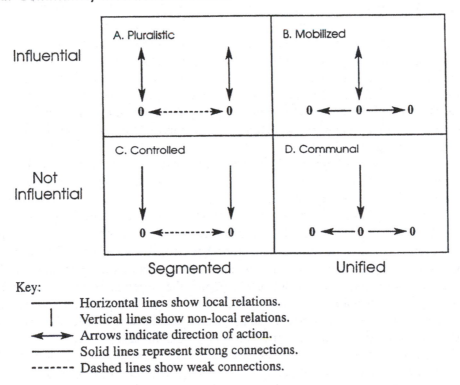

Key:

——— Horizontal lines show local relations.

| Vertical lines show non-local relations.

◄——► Arrows indicate direction of action.

——— Solid lines represent strong connections.

------- Dashed lines show weak connections.

The Elements of Community Organizing

Community organizing is planned attempts to alter neighborhood interactional patterns in order to make communities stronger and to solve community problems. Some organizers seek to move communities from segmented to unified, to remove the internal divisions among residents in a community that hinder their participation in local decision making. This strategy is called "locality development." Other organizers focus on the vertical pattern, wanting to make nonlocal resources more available to many communities. This strategy is called "coordinated planning." Still other organizers believe that changes in the vertical pattern are necessary, but insist that these changes cannot come from the top (nonlocal central offices) down. Instead, they insist on increasing the influence of the "grass roots," citizens in neighborhoods, on central actors. This organizing strategy is called "social action" (Bursik & Grasmick, 1993; Lyon, 1987).

Locality Development. Locality development is perceived by its adherents as a conscious attempt to unify the community by creating new, problem-solving bodies (councils, committees, and federations) within a community. When locality development is undertaken solely by local residents, "self-help" is an appropriate label for it. However, locality development is often conducted with professional organizing assistance from nonlocal organizations (e.g., Ford Foundation, HUD, the mayor's office). In either form, the hallmark of locality development is not solving particular problems (although specific problems will be addressed) but the creation and maintenance of local decision-making bodies. In other words, locality development is not a single-issue effort. The stress is on unifying the community. The community literature is not clear on the nature of the forces that can prevent unification. Some research suggests that differences among community members due to age, race, ethnicity, or class may make segmentation more likely, but other research suggests that these potential divisions of interest can be overcome with careful attention to conflict reduction and decision-making processes that integrate interests (Castells, 1983).

Coordinated Planning. Coordinated planning, which often includes technical assistance, is the most common strategy for community organizing. Coordinated planning focuses on applying nonlocal resources, expertise, and problem solving to a number of localities where, in the view of the expert, these applications are needed. Unlike locality development, planning may focus on a single issue (poverty, crime, housing) or address several related problems together. The initiator is nonlocal (e.g., city hall, state or federal government, a private foundation). While the initiators usually desire local participation, they often have already established priorities and problem-solving methods. They seek local participation in implementation rather than in design. Planning strategies also often prefer that local input go through preestablished channels set up by the nonlocal authority (Byrum, 1992; Warren, Rose & Bergunder, 1974). In other words, coordinated planning tends to stress what local organizations can do working with nonlocal organizations. It is less likely to stress direct involvement of residents.

While coordinated planning focuses on the vertical dimension of the community model, most planning efforts do not address the decision-making processes, or the structure of power, either within communities or between local and nonlocal groups. In most cases of coordinated planning, nonlocal authorities retain power as they seek to improve communities by applying new resources to local problems. Because of this tendency, planning seems to work best in localities that are already unified—that is, in areas where local problem-solving bodies exist that represent the whole community and can help to determine the appropriate use of new resources. When planners enter nonunified communities, they often end up taking sides in a divided area, whether they intend to or not.

Social Action. Social action is an organizing strategy that recognizes that dramatic community change generally involves changes in the power or decision-making structure of community. Social action has to do with equalizing power among unequals so that effective democratic bargaining and fair exchange may occur among the parties. Therefore, the essence of all social action is "bottom-up" influence, or grassroots decisionmaking. However, the most well-known and most effective social action strategies are not simply increased influence in the vertical dimension of community. Many social action organizers view communities as products of local and nonlocal forces (e.g., much like Figure 10.1) and they assume that both dimensions must be affected (Cortes, 1993; Reitzes & Reitzes, 1982). In other words, gaining influence will require some unification. Social action strategists, therefore, often employ a dual method, exerting influence on nonlocal organizations through social action, while bringing local people together through locality development (Delgado, 1986; Fish, 1973).

Unlike coordinated planning and locality development (used alone), social action is based on the assumption that, in effecting change, conflict will occur (Alinsky, 1969). Thus, disruptive tactics like picketing, strikes, and demonstrations are an important part of the social action strategy. The critics of social action (who are usually central-office types whose lives are made more difficult by the "rabble-rousers") often pick on these conflict tactics to show that social action is not "democratic." But at the same time that social action employs contest tactics with nonlocals, it employs highly participative, democratic tactics within the local unification effort. Moreover, the long-run aim is to collaborate with nonlocal central offices, not to replace them (Alinsky, 1969).

Obstacles to Community Organizing by Police

As city police departments try to engage communities in crime prevention and public safety efforts, they face several obstacles. These problems can be examined by looking at previous police involvement in community organizing and how the three organizing strategies were applied. (It is important to remember that the police and city government are both treated as nonlocal, central authorities in this discussion, because even local government is outside specific neighborhoods and must deal with several neighborhood communities at once.)

Police and Coordinated Planning. The bulk of criminal justice activities in community organizing consist of coordinated planning (no surprise here). For example, Neighborhood Watch, Drug Abuse Resistance Education (DARE), and Operation Weed and Seed are programs designed by nonlocal experts and recommended to the localities. The implementation chain is complex and incremental. The initiators generally cannot force compliance, but through accommodation, co-optation, and resource exchange, planners persuade people to comply. This filtering process has the tendency to transform programs, as envisioned by the planners, into something slightly different from the original plan in each instance of application.

Under pressure for accountability and efficiency, the initiators in coordinated planning will generally prefer to deal with established, reliable, and cooperative local organizations. This tendency may lead the initiating group to do more business with influential communities rather than noninfluential communities, or, within communities to favor more powerful (and friendlier) groups than others (for example, to favor homeowners over renters). Often coordinated planning efforts bypass the local community altogether and deal instead with individuals, such as by instructing individuals on how to avoid victimization (Bursik & Grasmick, 1993). When this happens, valuable services may be provided to individuals, but the process of community building does not occur. In other words, the planner did not help bring people together or help people become more influential.

Disappointing results from coordinated planning efforts have appeared time and again in evaluation studies, without discouraging the commitment of governments and foundations to try this form of organizing. While the expertise and resources located in nonlocal centers of power may be sorely needed in many communities, this technical know-how and resources to mount programs is more effective when the communities receiving the plan have gone through a process of locality development or social action first. When coordinated planning finds a way to connect with unified and influential local groups, then the resources available through planning are usually more effectively used, because local people have more capacity to participate in problem-solving efforts.

Police and Locality Development. Because locality development is not problem-specific, but rather an effort to increase community unification, it will be difficult for police executives to be the initiators of this process. When the neighborhood level problem-solving bodies only occasionally place crime-related issues on the table, the police may face internal doubts and external challenges to the legitimacy of their participation in these efforts (e.g., why are the police involved in non-police business?). However, if the police try to initiate locality development, their intervention typically leads to dependency on the police and to single-issue, or specialist organizations rather than to community unification (Bursik & Grasmick, 1993).

To deal with this dilemma, police could make their in-kind resources or funds available to support locality development by others, rather than trying to participate in all community decisions or trying to be the initiators. A difficulty with this support role, however, is that locality developers usually want to ascertain that no conditions or strings attach to the use of police resources (an unlikely commitment from police). Further, in some neighborhoods, taking resources or support from the police might diminish local unification, because some community members do not trust the police (often with good reason). Because of such dilemmas that face the police in locality development, the more effective police role might be as facilitator or contributor to specific projects undertaken by an existing neighborhood council or committee. For example, the police department may wish to assign an officer as a liaison to the local neighborhood association for public safety and crime prevention issues, rather than create a special crime prevention council that works with the police but not on other community issues.

If the police department adopts this supportive, consultative role, other difficulties arise. One is whether the police will be able to respond quickly and appropriately when they receive specific requests from different neighborhoods. Unless police decisionmaking is very decentralized and police resource allocation very flexible, neighborhood requests for assistance and police priorities and resource allocations may not fit together. The result, then, is that the community group encounters an unresponsive police agency (Bayley, 1994; Weingart, Hartmann & Osborne, 1994). Therefore, the department must learn how to scan communities and adapt to multiple and different requests from different places.

When citywide organizations such as the police do respond to requests from specific communities, equity across neighborhoods may also be of concern. For example, in Seattle other neighborhoods were concerned that the South Precinct received more than its share of police attention (NIJ, 1992). Because locality development processes will not occur at the same rate in all neighborhoods, and because not all neighborhood groups will simultaneously find crime an urgent issue, equitable resource allocation needs to be addressed continually. To the extent that police do accept an implementation rather than an initiator role, the department again faces the dilemma of supporting neighborhoods that already are unified rather than those that are segmented, although segmented communities may have greater crime problems. The department cannot work with a segmented community in the same way that it works with a unified one, but it must deal with crime in both kinds of places.

Police and Social Action. Police are more often a target than a collaborator in social action. Social action organizers often use disruptive tactics against nonlocal centers of power as a means of both initiating the unification process and increasing community influence, particularly in the early stages of organizing.

Police can become a target in several ways. Inflammatory police actions can arouse protest from a neighborhood and in this way promote community unification (although an angry reaction may not lead to sustained organizing). By contrast, police inaction or perceived ineffectiveness may also galvanize social action (Lyons, 1999; Weingart et al., 1994). More likely than either of these scenarios is one in which police become secondary targets when they are called on to protect the original target or to restore order during a conflict.

Responding to social action organizing may be the most delicate situation in which police executives may find themselves. This organizing may unify a community and make it more influential, and police should favor stronger communities. But police chiefs can support social action only if they are willing to tackle major ethical issues and assume considerable political risk. If police are targeted in a social action strategy, their natural response is coercive reassertion of authority. Indeed, some social action strategists would seek to provoke such a response because this visible police retaliation can lead to greater mobilization of the residents. From an organizer's point of view, therefore, a knee-jerk, coercive police response is not all bad, or is not always bad (Alinsky, 1969; Stoecker, 1994).

While mutually coercive interaction has some tactical value for social action, it also has limits. Social action organizers often realize that they may need police cooperation later, against other targets (such as drug dealers or absentee, exploitive landlords). This is the typical dilemma in poor, minority neighborhoods where greater protection from crime and greater fairness and respect from the police are both issues. They also know that either the disruptive tactics, such as picketing, or the police retaliation to those tactics may deter some potential neighborhood recruits from participating (Delgado, 1986). Consequently, one challenge to police leaders (and social action leaders) is to find creative and productive responses to citizen anger and find ways to involve the agency in social action mobilization without diffusing citizen initiative and commitment to public action (Comer, 1985; Weingart et al., 1994).

Subtle Resistance to Community Building

The greatest threat to community improvement is never getting it off the ground because institutionalized beliefs and behaviors prevent it (Warren et al., 1974). The police may contribute to this problem. They might, for example, approach community frustrations with neighborhood drug dealing by instructing the neighborhood group to leave the problem to the police. They might deal with legitimate grievances against other nonlocal centers of power by carting off to jail people who protest against those powers or by making it impossible for them to protest (Weingart et al., 1994). But if the police are seen as sympathetic to the neighborhood residents in their struggle with politically powerful actors, those actors will accuse the police of favoritism or even of giving in to crime and disorder.

Probably the most powerful influence that the police may have in retarding community building is completely unintended. They may contribute to preventing change by concentrating the attention of the community on immediate and local sources of crime and disorder at the risk of long-term solutions that deal with nonlocal and indirect sources of community decay (Cortes, 1993; DeLeon-Granados, 1999; Lyons, 1999; Skogan, 1990).

Consider the sources of crime in a neighborhood drug market. These sources may be visible and local, but the impact of economic development policies that favor downtown business and suburban growth over neighborhood revitalization is invisible and indirect (Byrum, 1992). If policing diverts attention from rather than complements attacks on these larger problems, it could do more harm than good, particularly in segmented and noninfluential communities. Because social action strategists usually recognize the importance of these nonlocal forces on communities, they may be reluctant to engage in or be suspicious of crime reduction efforts (DeLeon-Granados, 1999; Hope, 1995, Skogan 1988).

The limitations and dilemmas imposed on police agencies, if they are to be involved in social action, are challenging. As a result, police may prefer coordinated planning as their strategy of choice, with locality development as their back-up or second choice. But community organizers and community researchers alike agree that social action coupled with locality development in a dual strategy is the most effective strategy in communities that face the greatest probability of crime and disorder (DeLeon-Granados, 1999; Lyons, 1999). If police are to achieve real progress in community crime prevention, community policing, or other approaches that engage communities in social control, they will have to tackle these knotty issues head-on. The police will have to find ways to support locality development without co-opting it into a narrow crime specialty. They will have to find a way to support social action without asking for "partners" who never criticize or exercise independent judgment.

Conclusion

Problems and Responses

This review of community organizing strategies and the involvement of police agencies in them can be summed up in a series of problems and suggested responses. The responses, which are presented as recommendations to police chiefs, reflect ways in which various interactions can be changed to support more effective crime reduction.

Problem 1: The police focus on community too often examines only local (e.g., residents in the neighborhood) relationships.
Response: Chiefs must learn to recognize that all communities are dynamic products of local and nonlocal interactions (including nonlocal forces such as large corporate interests and other units of government that may have a vested interest in keeping certain policies harmful to poor neighborhoods off the table).

Problem 2: The history of prior community organizing indicates that increased access to nonlocal resources (such as more services) is not sufficient and may actually hinder the process of strengthening many communities. Communities need more influence, not merely more help.

Response: Chiefs must recognize that communities need a voice in the determination of what resources to use and how to use them. In neighborhoods where there is no organized voice, help must wait on the reorganization of the neighborhood. Chiefs may be able to assist in the reorganization process, but this requires a consultative, facilitative role, not a "take charge and do it" role. Solving a specific problem is less important than developing an ongoing problem-solving capacity in a neighborhood.

Problem 3: The strengths and weaknesses of community organizing strategies depend on the fit between what is tried and where. Chiefs may inappropriately seek to apply what worked successfully elsewhere to a neighborhood with different characteristics.

Response: Executives must learn to assess all organizing options in terms of the specific community dynamics (the interactional field) in a particular place at a particular time. There is no reason to trust or distrust local or nonlocal initiatives simply because of where they originated, but there is no reason to trust that a "model" program built in one location works everywhere.

Problem 4: Improving order and stability in a community is not necessarily the same thing as favoring what appear to be the forces of order in the current situation. For example, siding with homeowners or business owners against bored and noisy teenagers may appear to be siding with order, but it may not contribute to building a more unified community.

Response: Organizing a neighborhood entails disorganizing its current interactional field. The presence of conflict must be evaluated strategically; simply reacting to the behavior of those who appear to be "in the wrong" can make the situation worse (see Chapter 12). Can "trouble-makers" become problem-solvers?

Problem 5: Planning crime-control activities and developing communities that can control crime are different processes. Orchestrating a citywide plan is not the same as encouraging community organizations with their own initiatives. Large organizations with citywide responsibility, even if decentralized, often pressure neighborhood organizations that they are trying to help to imitate bureaucratic and professional norms and structures that stifle innovation and participation, and keep the city department in control.

Response: Police chiefs need to create units and officer behaviors that can provide assistance without assuming control; assist neighborhood groups to network with each other, locally and nationally; scan neighborhoods continuously, not merely for problems, but for new strengths. Reward and encourage those strengths as they emerge; do not expect fledgling organizations to mirror the internal control and accounting systems imposed on the city organization.

Problem 6: Strengthening many neighborhoods, especially controlled communities, is likely to set off an expression of anger and resentment and the use of disruptive tactics within the neighborhood as it seeks to gain influence. Such tactics are likely to cause backlash from established groups and organizations.

Response: Chiefs sympathetic to community building will need to protect their own officers who collaborate with neighborhoods in this process. They also need to promote, not quiet, criticism of the department and learn to use that criticism for improvement. If you do not hear about your mistakes, you cannot improve.

Problem 7: Doing the police part to promote community is insufficient. Indeed, relying on criminal justice agencies and resources to promote community, *absent other changes in the city*, is likely to maintain long-term dependence of and control over poor neighborhoods. Very frankly, it is a sham.

Response: Responsible police leadership includes clear and aggressive statements about the contributions expected of other public and private organizations. Do not give politicians and financial leaders the opportunity to behave as if community building is the sole domain of the police (or the criminal justice system). Although law enforcement and other criminal justice agencies may serve as the catalyst for community building, other public and private agencies, financial institutions, citizen groups, and neighborhood associations must all work together to create community.

References

Alinsky, S. (1969). *Reveille for Radicals*. New York, NY: Vintage.

Bayley, D.H. (1994). *Policing for the Future*. New York, NY: Oxford University Press.

Bursik, R.J., and H. Grasmick (1993). *Neighborhoods and Crime: The Dimensions of Effective Crime Control*. New York, NY: Lexington Books.

Byrum, O.E. (1992). *Old Problems in New Times: Urban Strategies for the 1990s*. Chicago, IL: Planners Press.

Castells, M. (1983). *The City and the Grassroots*. Berkeley, CA: University of California Press.

Comer, J.P. (1985). "Black Violence and Public Policy." In L.A. Curtis (ed.), *American Violence and Public Policy: An Update of the National Commission on the Causes and Prevention of Violence*. New Haven, CT: Yale University Press.

Cortes, E. (1993). "Reweaving the Fabric: The Iron Rule and the IAF Strategy for Dealing with Poverty through Power and Politics." Piscataway, NJ: Rutgers University Center for Urban Policy Research, Working Paper 56.

DeLeon-Granados, W. (1999). *Travels Through Crime and Place*. Boston, MA: Northeastern University Press.

Delgado, G. (1986). *Organizing the Movement: The Roots and Growth of ACORN*. Philadelphia, PA: Temple University Press.

Fish, J.H. (1973). *Black Power, White Control: The Struggle of the Woodlawn Organization in Chicago*. Princeton, NJ: Princeton University Press.

Hallman, H.W. (1984). *Neighborhoods: Their Place in Urban Life*. Beverly Hills, CA: Sage Publications.

Hope, T. (1995). "Community Crime Prevention." In M. Tonry and D.P. Farrington (eds.), *Building a Safer Society*. Chicago: University of Chicago Press.

Langworthy, R.H., and L.F. Travis III (eds.) (1994). *Policing in America: A Balance of Forces*. New York, NY: Macmillan.

Lyon, L. (1987). *The Community in Urban Society*. Philadelphia, PA: Temple University Press.

Lyons, W. (1999). *The Politics of Community Policing: Rearranging the Power to Punish*. Ann Arbor, MI: University of Michigan Press.

National Institute of Justice (1992). "Community Policing in Seattle: A Model Partnership between Citizens and Police." *NIJ Research in Brief*. Washington, DC: National Institute of Justice.

Rabrenovic, G. (1996). *Community-Builders*. Philadelphia, PA: Temple University Press.

Reitzes, D.C., and D.C. Reitzes (1982). "Alinsky Reconsidered: A Reluctant Community Theorist." *Social Science Quarterly*, 63:256-279.

Skogan, W.G. (1990). *Disorder and Decline: Crime and the Spiral of Decay in American Urban Neighborhoods*. Berkeley, CA: University of California Press.

_____ (1988). "Community Organizations and Crime." In M. Tonry and N. Morris (eds.) *Crime and Justice, A Review of Research*, Volume 10. Chicago, IL: University of Chicago Press.

Skogan, W.G., and M.G. Maxfield (1981). *Coping with Crime: Individual and Neighborhood Reactions*. Beverly Hills, CA: Sage Publications.

Spergel, I.A. (1976). *Politics, Policies, and the Delinquent Problem*. Glenrock, NJ: Microfilm Corp. of America.

Stoecker, R. (1994). *Defending Community: The Struggle for Alternative Redevelopment in Cedar-Riverside*. Philadelphia, PA: Temple University Press.

Warren, R.L. (1978). *Community in America*, Third Edition. Chicago, IL: Rand-McNally.

Warren, R.L., S.M. Rose, and A.F. Bergunder (1974). *The Structure of Urban Reform: Community Decision Organizations in Stability and Change*. Lexington, MA: Lexington Books.

Weingart, S.N., F.X. Hartmann, and D. Osborne (1994). "Case Studies of Community Anti-Drug Efforts." *NIJ Research in Brief*. Washington, DC: U.S. Department of Justice.

The Benefits
of Community Policing
in Rural Oklahoma   11

Michael W. Brand
University of Oklahoma

Michael L. Birzer
Washburn University

Introduction

Community policing continues to be the driving force for change in American policing. Many police agencies—large and small, urban and rural—have implemented key features of community policing. Community policing infers internal, organizational change. At the same time, community policing strategies have been applied with the externally focused goals of detecting and preventing crime. Furthermore, in light of the fact that many agencies received federal expenditures as part of the 1994 Crime Bill to implement community policing strategies, the need for evaluations of community policing practices in many American cities and rural areas in particular is apparent.

Background and Setting

This paper reports the results of a survey that assessed community policing in a small town in Oklahoma.[1] Choteau is a rural farming community located in northeastern Oklahoma with a population of about 1,500 residents. Choteau has experienced significant population growth over the past several years. Due in part to the growth of families and individuals moving from Tulsa's more urban environment, drug trafficking has increased through the use of secondary highways to transport drugs in and around the Choteau area. Law enforcement officials in Choteau believed they began to see an increase in drug use and drug-related crimes several years ago. As a result, local law enforcement officials started to look for ways to combat this trend in drug use and related crime. Furthermore, they were interested in identifying strategies that would nurture long-lasting community partnerships.

---

[1] This research stemmed from a Problem-Solving Partnership Grant through the United States Department of Justice, ORI: OK043901.

The Choteau Police Department is a small police agency with five full-time police officers and four reserve police officers. Like many police agencies across the United States, the Choteau Police Department received a community policing/problem-solving partnership grant from the Department of Justice in the mid-1990s. Choteau police officials saw the grant as a resource that would help them to evolve into more of a proactive, problem-solving department, which they historically had not been.

Researchers were invited to assess public perceptions of crime, citizen perceptions of the police department, perceptions of the quality of police service, and perceptions of general community maintenance issues. Data from pre- and post-surveys were examined, and general comparisons were made regarding public perceptions before and after the implementation of community policing. Another interest was to determine what factors accounted for the success of community policing. Researchers were instructed to specifically look at important aspects of community policing related to informing and engaging community members in public safety, including increasing the number of favorable contacts between the police and the community.

In 1998, the Choteau Police Department formally implemented some of the key strategies of community policing into their operations. These strategies included problem solving, partnerships with business, drug education and awareness, increased neighborhood prevention programs, and more contact and communication with the community. Prior to this intervention, 1,200 adult residents were mailed surveys designed to measure citizens' perception of the police department, quality of police services, citizen safety perceptions, and general areas of concern. In all, 299 surveys (25 percent) were returned.

Two years after the Choteau Police Department had implemented community policing, a follow-up survey was mailed to the same population of local residents. Of these 1,200 surveys, 275 surveys (23 percent) were returned. This follow-up survey asked respondents the same questions as the previous survey administered prior to the implementation of community policing.

Key Issues

In both surveys, citizens were given a list of 14 areas of possible concern and asked to rate each concern as a major problem, minor problem, no problem, or don't know. Among the areas that were reported as major concerns, their respective percentage in the pre-community policing survey were: vandalism (56 percent), abandoned vehicles (60 percent), drug use (41 percent), drug dealing (41 percent).

The same concerns were presented to citizens two years after the implementation of community policing. Citizens were again asked to rate each concern as a major problem, minor problem, no problem, or don't know. The results suggested that considerable improvements in public safety had occurred.

Recall the results of the pre-community policing survey, in which 56 percent of the citizens reported vandalism as a major concern. The second survey revealed that only 44 percent of the citizens thought vandalism was a major concern. Sixty percent of the citizens in the pre-community policing survey reported abandoned vehicles to be a major concern compared with only nine percent in the post-community policing survey. Forty-one percent of the respondents reported drug use as a major concern in the pre-community policing survey, compared to only 23 percent in the post-community policing survey. Forty-one percent reported drug dealing to be a major problem in the pre-community policing survey and only 19 percent reported it to be a problem in the post-community policing survey.

A few other areas of interest were general order-maintenance issues. For example, in the pre-community policing survey, 15 percent of the respondents reported public drinking as a major concern compared to only six percent in the post-community policing survey. Twelve percent of the respondents in the pre-community policing survey reported youth hanging out to be a major concern compared to only seven percent in the post-community policing survey. Twenty-two percent of the citizens reported unsupervised youth to be a major problem on the pre-community survey compared to only 11 percent on the post-community policing survey.

Citizen Safety Issues

Both the pre-community policing survey and the post-community policing survey asked citizens to rate safety concerns in their neighborhoods. Specifically, citizens were asked to rate whether they felt very safe, somewhat safe, somewhat unsafe, or very unsafe in their neighborhood at night and while driving at night. Regarding the question that asked citizens if they felt safe in their neighborhood at night, 43 percent in the pre-community policing survey reported feeling very unsafe compared to only two percent on the post-community policing survey. Fifty-four percent of the citizens reported feeling very safe while driving at night in the pre-community policing survey compared to 63 percent on the post-community policing survey.

Quality of Police Services

Both the pre- and post-community policing surveys asked citizens to rate the police department. Specifically, citizens were asked to rate police as excellent, good, acceptable, or poor on several categories. The first item asked citizens how well the police did on satisfying their calls for services. In the pre-community policing survey 23 percent of the citizens responded that the police did an excellent job. In the post-community policing survey 30 percent of the citizens thought the police had done an excellent job in this respect. In 1998, Choteau residents rated the overall police department performance as follows: 33 percent excellent, 39 percent good, 16 percent acceptable, eight percent poor, and three percent said they did not know. Two years later, after the implementation of community policing, Choteau residents gave the police department the following marks: 39 percent excellent, 42 percent good, nine percent acceptable, six percent poor, and three percent reported they did not know.

Citizen Involvement

In the pre- and post-community policing surveys, Choteau residents also were asked to indicate their awareness and interest in crime watch programs and neighborhood associations. Prior to the implementation of community policing, citizens in Choteau had limited knowledge of neighborhood watch programs and neighborhood associations. The police department began to offer informational sessions on neighborhood watch programs, and two years after the implementation of community policing some 67 percent of citizens completing our survey indicated they would most definitely be interested in establishing a neighborhood watch program. Similarly, when residents were informed about neighborhood associations, 47 percent indicated they would be willing to participate in a neighborhood association.

Police Activities

Radio calls and activities that Choteau police officers were engaged in both prior to the implementation of community policing and then again one year after implementation were analyzed. During the year prior to the implementation of community policing, Choteau police officers investigated 127 cases of domestic violence, 38 cases of burglary, 123 cases of suspicious persons, 15 cases of underage drinking, 215 juvenile calls, and 12 shoplifter complaints. Two years after the implementation of community policing these same calls were significantly reduced: 103 cases of domestic violence, 15 cases of burglary, 71 cases of suspicious persons, two cases of underage drinking, 112 juvenile calls, and three shoplifter complaints.

Self-Initiated Activity

During the year prior to the implementation of community policing, Choteau police officers engaged in numerous self-initiated activities. Three activities discussed here help explain the positive results experienced in the reduction of radio calls and cases. Similarly, these self-initiated activities also may be partly responsible for favorable ratings by citizens of the police department. The following self-initiated activities were recorded the year prior to the implementation of community policing: 65 field contacts, 59 welfare checks, and 43 building checks. One year after the implementation of community policing, Choteau police officers engaged in these same initiated activities as follows: 152 field contacts, 636 welfare checks, and 98 building checks. These stark increases in self-initiated contacts likely explain the reduction in burglary calls, juvenile calls, and calls involving youth, such as underage drinking, due to increased contact between the police and the community.

Discussion

It would appear that the Choteau Police Department has experienced favorable results with community policing. Areas of major concern that citizens reported prior to the implementation of community policing, such as public drinking, youth hanging out, vandalism, abandoned vehicles, drug use, and drug dealing, were significantly reduced as major concerns two years after the implementation of community policing. Citizen perceptions of safety also were significantly changed in a more favorable light. For example, prior to the implementation of community policing, 43 percent of the citizens reported feeling very unsafe in their neighborhood at night compared to only two percent two years after the implementation of community policing. Furthermore, 54 percent of the citizens reported feeling very safe driving at night prior to the implementation of community policing. However, two years after the implementation of community policing, some 63 percent of the citizens reported that they felt very safe while driving at night. Once again, we think this may be due in part to the increased number of general field contacts and welfare checks made by the police department.

The citizens rated the quality of police service significantly higher after the implementation of community policing. It also was readily apparent that citizens became more aware of the existence of neighborhood crime prevention programs and neighborhood associations two years after the implementation of community policing. This may be due in part to the mobilization of the community through community meetings and an increase in media announcements.

We point to several other factors that may be largely responsible for the positive results of community policing in Choteau. The police department worked closely with the public schools to increase their presence on campus as well as increasing the rate and frequency of K-9 patrols during school hours. School and police department officials jointly attended alcohol abuse prevention training programs. This may explain the reduction in the citizen concerns about drug use and drug dealing. Furthermore, the police department began to collaborate with many private agencies. Historically in Choteau this had not been done to a great extent. The police department also worked closely with local businesses to help raise funds to purchase alcohol and drug abuse prevention material for use in the public school. Finally, the police increased personal contacts with local businesses and established a more personalized rapport.

One other factor we feel is significant in the positive results reported here is that the police department formed partnerships and worked with residents, businesses, and city maintenance to increase visibility and safety around intersections. This was a concern of residents in the past, and it was feared that many intersections were prone to traffic accidents because of traffic law violators. Additionally, police officers worked to decrease the number of abandoned vehicles left for sale in parking lots and alongside the road. This was accomplished by the city initiating a permit requirement in order for citizens to leave vehicles for sale or abandoned in parking lots or along the road. The Choteau Police Department hosted several meetings for residents in which alcohol and drug prevention materials were presented. In addition to the educational activities, the department initiated efforts to increase personal contact with residents. The department also began to more effectively deploy its reserve (volunteer) officers on evening and weekend shifts to increase contact and presence in the community through foot patrol. This is important in that developing interpersonal and cooperative interaction between citizens and the police is what may very well be the cornerstone of community policing (see Kratcoski & Dukes, 1995; Andranovich, 1997).

The police in a community policing environment are frequently expected to not only respond to the full range of problems that the public expects the police to handle, including peacekeeping, but also to take the initiative to identify broader community needs and problems that may affect the public's sense of well-being (Goldstein, 1987). The Choteau Police Department went beyond the traditional police duties and concentrated on community concerns such as abandoned vehicles and general neighborhood maintenance issues. Such an approach fits with the published community policing literature regarding what community policing means to police executives and the communities they serve (see Alpert & Dunham, 1992; Carter & Radelet, 1999; LaGrange, 1998; Peak & Glensor, 1996; Zhao & Thurman, 1997).

Challenges

While community policing represents a new way of thinking for the Choteau Police Department, it also appears to be effective. Over the course of the two years the grant project has been in place, the department and community have met many challenges. One such challenge has been staff turnover and the need to reeducate officers in community policing. Currently, it appears that the leadership within the police department supports and understands the underpinnings of community policing. Second, while it appears that the department initially viewed the COPS grant as a way of increasing resources, eventually the department became more comfortable with this new approach. Community policing conferences sponsored by the Justice Department appeared to be of significant help in making this transition.

Several other significant challenges faced throughout the grant period included the ability to gather and organize the necessary data, mustering the resources and knowledge to analyze the data, and the ability to involve the community in the process. These challenges do not appear to be unique to Choteau, and many small rural police departments would seem to welcome assistance with these facets of a grant program. In this respect, the University of Oklahoma's Center for Economic Development and East Central University's Department of Human Resources played a significant role in assisting Choteau with the implementation of the grant. However, as the data suggest, with the proper support the Choteau Police Department was able to make the shift to community policing and implement significant, lasting changes within their community.

Conclusion

Many rural communities possess the interest, motivation, and existing community networks that are necessary for the successful implementation of community policing. Once implemented, these types of initiatives allow rural police departments the ability to initiate changes in policing procedures that will have lasting and highly favorable effects in their communities.

References

Alpert, G.P., and R.G. Dunham (1992). *Policing Urban America*, Second Edition. Prospect Heights, IL: Waveland Press, Inc.

Andranovich, G. (1997). "Organizing and Managing Community Policing: Collaborative Problem Solving Outside the Agency." In Q.C. Thurman and E.F. McGarrell (eds.), *Community Policing in a Rural Setting*, Cincinnati, OH: Anderson Publishing Co.

Carter, D.L., and L.A. Radelet (1999). *The Police and the Community*, Sixth Edition. Upper Saddle River, NJ: Prentice Hall.

Goldstein, H. (1987, December). "The New Policing: Confronting Complexity." *NIJ Research in Brief*. Washington, DC: National Institute of Justice.

Kratcoski, P.C., and D. Dukes (1995). *Issues in Community Policing*. Cincinnati, OH: Anderson Publishing Co.

LaGrange, R.L. (1998). *Policing American Society*, Second Edition. Chicago, IL: Nelson-Hall.

Oliver, W.M. (1998). *Community Oriented Policing: A Systematic Approach to Policing*. Upper Saddle River, NJ: Prentice Hall.

Peak, K.J., and R.W. Glensor (1996). *Community Policing and Problem Solving: Strategies and Practices*. Upper Saddle River, NJ: Prentice Hall.

Zhao, J., and Q.C. Thurman (1997). "Facilitators and Obstacles to Community Policing in a Rural Setting." In Q.C. Thurman and E.F. McGarrell (eds.), *Community Policing in a Rural Setting*, Cincinnati, OH: Anderson Publishing Co.

Getting to Know Your Community Through Citizen Surveys and Focus Group Interviews 12

Edmund F. McGarrell
Michigan State University

Socorro Benitez
Eastern Washington University

Ricky S. Gutierrez
California State University—Sacramento

....

Community policing involves the development of police-citizen partnerships to identify and solve neighborhood problems, with the goal being the co-production of safe and orderly communities and the enhancement of the quality of community life. A key element for law enforcement in creating such partnerships is to develop an understanding of this "partner." This chapter discusses two methods of developing this understanding—the community survey and the focus group interview.

There are a number of reasons for conducting surveys and focus group interviews with community members. Three are highlighted here. First, the information generated can assist in a performance appraisal of the organization. Traditional indicators of police performance, such as offenses known and arrests, have long been recognized as flawed, at least if considered uncritically. Do increased "offenses known" indicate poor police performance, or are the police being successful in convincing citizens to report their victimizations? Do increased arrests indicate good policing or rising crime? The community survey and focus group interviews can provide direct information on police performance from the agency's customers. A second goal of the community survey and focus group interviews is to support problem-solving activities within the community and to help set police priorities. Third, the community survey and focus groups can be used as part of an evaluation of specific programs.

Key Issues

This chapter draws on the experience of the Washington State Institute for Community Oriented Policing (WSICOP) in working with a number of law enforcement agencies, primarily in the state of Washington, and including rural, small-town, and medium-sized urban cities. Samples of the survey instrument and focus group questions are included as Appendices C and D. Although adapted to the specific agency and community, the surveys generally cover the following topics:

- assessment of the level and quality of police services
- fear of crime
- victimization experience
- neighborhood crime and disorder problems
- police-public relations
- assessment of and support for community policing

The chapter first introduces some of the technical issues that need to be addressed in conducting a community survey. We then present examples of how the survey can be used to serve the objectives of performance appraisal, problem solving, and program evaluation. We end by turning to the topic of the focus group interview. Again, issues related to actually conducting focus group interviews are discussed along with some of the reasons for using focus groups and examples demonstrating their use.

Discussion

Conducting the Community Survey

As was mentioned in Chapter 8, law enforcement executives planning a community survey may wish to work with a local college or university. Three sets of issues will need to be addressed: topics to be covered and specific survey items; sampling; and method of survey administration. In terms of topics to be covered and specific items, there are a number of benefits to creating a vertical survey team, perhaps including community members, to brainstorm about topics to be covered in the survey. The survey team will need to consider the purposes for conducting the survey, who will complete the survey, and how long it will take to complete. The WSICOP survey is included as Appendix C to provide an example of some of the topics covered in surveys by various law enforcement agencies. The discussion that follows in this chapter focuses primarily on the substance of these surveys.

Sampling is an extremely important topic to resolve. Even in the smallest community, it is likely to be inefficient and costly to attempt to survey all the members of the community. Years of survey sampling research have demonstrated that a properly selected sample can provide as accurate a picture of community opinion as can a survey of the entire population. Thus, a survey of 500 to 800 residents can potentially provide an accurate picture of the citizens of your community.

The key here is to have a randomly selected sample. In WSICOP's experience with law enforcement agencies, often the first thought in proposing a community survey is to rely on what researchers call a convenience sample. This might include a day at the mall where selected citizens are asked a set of questions, or perhaps a survey of all the department's civilian volunteers. The problem with such convenience samples is that they are inherently biased. They only provide a picture of the attitudes of the citizens who potentially could have been selected under the given method (e.g., all citizens at the mall on a given day who walk by the area where the survey takers are standing).

The goal in the random sample is that every member of the target population have the same, or known, likelihood of being selected for participation. One popular method is to use a phone survey employing random digit dialing. Computer programs exist to randomly dial phone numbers in a given jurisdiction. This produces a representative sample of all phone numbers in the jurisdiction. Because the vast majority of households in contemporary society have telephones, most researchers consider this an acceptable form of sampling (it may cause problems, however, if a sizable proportion of households do not have phones). If a mail survey is being planned, then a sampling frame, a list of all addresses in the jurisdiction, must be assembled. Commercial services are available that can provide such lists. Additionally, several computerized services that can generate a list of names and addresses for all households with telephones are now available. The key question in the use of such services is how complete a coverage of the local jurisdiction the service provides.

The third key issue is whether to conduct a phone or mail survey (a third option is the more expensive face-to-face interview, which is conducted by knocking on doors and interviewing people firsthand). The advantage of phone surveys is that they typically generate a high response rate (with adequate calls back when no one is home or the line is busy). The disadvantage is that they usually are more expensive because of the interviewer time involved. The mail survey offers the advantage of convenience to the respondent—they can complete the survey when they so desire. Also, more complex questions can be asked because the respondent has time to think through the question and his or her answer (although a danger is that there is no interviewer to provide explanation). The disadvantage is that they take quite a bit of work to obtain an acceptable response rate. In some of the communities WSICOP has worked with, it has been necessary to mail a reminder card, three follow-up surveys, and place a reminder phone call asking the respondent to please complete the survey, in order to generate an acceptable response rate (for a thorough discussion of these issues, see Dillman, 1978).

The point in this discussion is simply to highlight some of the key issues that need to be addressed in carrying out a valid community survey. At least initially, until in-house capacity is created, law enforcement agencies are likely to benefit greatly by collaborating with an experienced survey researcher in conducting the community survey.

Three Uses of the Community Survey

Performance Appraisal. Measuring the performance of public organizations like police departments and sheriff's agencies is difficult. Unlike private firms, there is no clear and unambiguous bottom line. Yet performance measurement is crucial to "reassure the public that hard-earned tax dollars [are] being spent to achieve important results and to hold police managers accountable for improving organizational performance" (Alpert & Moore, 1993:110). The community survey, particularly if repeated over time, offers a number of potential performance measures. Given that police managers cannot look at a profit statement to assess performance, the community survey offers a direct mechanism for assessing customer satisfaction.

One set of measures in the WSICOP survey asks the general question: What is your opinion of the quality of police services and the level of police services? In Spokane, Washington, where the police department has now completed three waves of community surveys (1992, 1994, 1995), 62 percent of the citizens in 1995 rated police services as good to excellent. This represented an eight percent increase over 1992, with a corresponding decline in the percent of citizens rating police services as poor. Even higher percentages of citizens in the small towns of Ellensburg and Moses Lake, Washington, rated their departments as good to excellent.

In addition to general ratings, more focused performance measures can also be included in the community survey. An important area for the quality of community life is fear of crime. The WSICOP survey includes two items that measure fear of crime. One item asks "how safe do you feel walking alone during the day in your neighborhood?" The second repeats the question but focuses on night rather than day. Because these items have been used in national survey samples, communities can compare themselves to other populations. Again, however, the real value is as an indicator of performance over time. For example, in Spokane, the percent of citizens reporting that they feel unsafe in their neighborhoods at night declined from 43 to 28 percent from 1992 to 1995. There was a 10 percent increase in the proportion feeling safe.

Another sign of performance is the percent of victims of crime who decide to report the offense to the police. The measurement of victimization in the citizen survey is tricky. Particularly with respect to serious violent offenses, which are rare occurrences, very large samples are needed to provide good measures. However, with this limitation in mind, citizens can be asked if they have been victimized and, if so, whether they reported the victimization. In Spokane there was a 16 percent increase from 1992 to 1995 in the percent of victims who reported their offense to the police. There was, indeed, an increase in reported crime in Spokane during this period, as official crime reports show. The increase in victim reporting uncovered in the community survey suggests that at least a portion of the increase in crime may not have been attributable to increasing crime or poor policing. Rather, it may have reflected the effect on citizens of the community policing message about the need to work with the police to solve neighborhood crime problems.

Problem Solving. Community surveys also provide information that can be used to assist in problem-solving activities and in setting agency priorities. The community survey in Ellensburg, Washington, surprised some members of the police department by revealing that the problem of most concern to citizens was drunk driving. In contrast, in Moses Lake, a town about the same size as Ellensburg, burglary, vandalism, and robbery were top concerns. Burglary, vandalism, drugs, and drunk driving were all highly rated problems in Spokane County, Washington. Citizen views on crime problems often differ from what law enforcement executives and line officers might think.

In a larger city, if sufficient numbers of respondents are included in the survey, the responses can be broken down by neighborhood for a better picture of problems facing citizens living in the same area. In the city of Spokane, responses were broken down by the city's 20 neighborhoods. One pattern that clearly emerged was that neighborhoods with high levels of reported fear also tended to have high levels of perceived disorder problems (e.g., drinking in public, teens hanging out and harassing other people, illegal drug use, and physical decay). This suggested targeted approaches to addressing disorder problems. In other neighborhoods, with low crime and disorder problems as reported by citizens, traffic was often considered the top neighborhood problem. The data clearly indicated that the problems and the corresponding responses to these problems needed to be tailored to the neighborhood.

Community surveys also can be used to explore community preferences for responses to various problems. For example, in Ellensburg, the survey revealed that citizens were strongly in favor of increased foot and bicycle patrol. Chief Hal Rees used this information to build expanded foot and bicycle patrol into the budget for the following year.

Program Evaluation. Related to the use of surveys for performance appraisal, the survey also can be used as part of an evaluation of a specific program. For example, the citizen survey shown in the Appendix could be administered to citizens who had attended the department's citizen academy. Particularly if administered before and after participation in the academy, the survey could indicate whether the program was providing information to participants and whether it led to better impressions of the police.

In Spokane, researchers at WSICOP have been involved in an evaluation of a fear, crime, and disorder reduction program in public housing. The research team conducted a series of interviews with residents of the public housing facility. The interviews were fashioned after the general community survey used by the police department. Among other findings, fear among residents of the public housing facility dropped dramatically and attitudes toward the police improved greatly. During the comparable period there was very little change on these dimensions among the citizens of Spokane generally. This lent credence to the interpretation that the program did indeed reduce fear and help improve resident-police relations.

Focus Group Interviews

The focus group interview approach was described in Chapter 8, and readers are directed to that discussion for information on the nature of focus groups. In this section, we concentrate on the use of focus group interviews with members of the public.

The Value of Focus Groups with Citizens. The reasons for conducting focus group interviews with citizens are similar to those for conducting focus groups with employees of the agency. Where the full-blown citizen survey is impractical, due to time or budgetary restrictions, focus group interviews can provide a timely and less costly "pulse of the community." Where the citizen survey has been conducted, the focus group can provide a means for exploring citizen attitudes, perceptions, and expectations in more depth than is possible with a survey instrument by itself.

Focus groups also can be used to tap into the perceptions of specialized subgroups within the community. For example, for concerns about delinquency and school-based violence or drug use, focus groups could be conducted with teachers, students, and parents. In Spokane, which has a relatively small but diverse non-white population, mail surveys generate very low response rates from African-American and Hispanic citizens. The police department, however, was very interested in the perceptions of these citizens. Consequently, a series of focus group interviews were conducted with members of these groups.

The focus group interview can also be a valuable component of program evaluation. In studying the fear, crime, and disorder reduction program in public housing mentioned above, focus groups were conducted with residents of the public housing facility as well as with area business owners, neighborhood-based police officers, housing authority staff, and others participating in the program. In addition to the goal of developing information about the perceptions, attitudes, and expectations of the agency's customers, the focus group interview, like the survey, demonstrates to the public that the police or sheriff's department cares about the opinions of its citizens.

Some Examples of Focus Group Findings. In two Washington communities, one a small urban city, the other a small agricultural town, focus group interviews were conducted as a follow-up to citizen surveys. The focus group participants were selected from groups within the population that were underrepresented in the survey. In both communities, members of the African-American and Hispanic communities expressed concern about crime and less familiarity with local law enforcement. Yet in both communities the focus group participants expressed high levels of interest in working with the police to solve local problems.

In a mid-sized western Washington community, focus groups were used to review perceptions of crime and the police in one section of the city that was experiencing high levels of crime. The focus group results proved enlightening to the police department, whose members expressed surprise at the amount of community support for innovative police-neighborhood strategies and the willingness of citizens to work with the police. As a consequence, a police ministation was opened in the neighborhood.

In another, though smaller, western Washington community, focus groups were conducted with area teenagers. Although this department was also surprised by the findings, in this case the surprise was of a more negative nature. Youths noted that they felt disrespect from the police and that the police had a negative image among their peers. Almost all of the contacts between youths and the police were described as negative. Although not pleasant to hear initially, these results forced the department to look at itself and formed the basis for efforts to improve relations between law enforcement and the youth of the community.

Focus Group Sampling. One of the trickiest issues in the focus group process is participant selection. For some purposes this is not a major concern. For example, in program evaluation, it may be possible to conduct focus group sessions with all relevant program participants. For many purposes, however, there is a larger pool of potential participants than could be included in focus group sessions and, often, there is no complete list of potential participants from which to sample. The typical response to this situation is to rely on convenience samples, and frequently these convenience samples contain clear biases. For example, in one community, the police generated a list of African-Americans who had attended the citizen's academy. A community leader and frequent critic of the police constructed a separate list of African-American citizens. The focus group interviews indicated tremendous support for the police among the first group and significant distrust of the police among the second. Although both "voices" are important, these convenience samples did not provide a clear picture of the general African-American community as a whole. Such an example illustrates the danger of convenience samples. Discerning "truth" from either sample could lead to wildly inaccurate estimations about support and distrust, and ultimately lead problem solving to wrong-headed solutions.

Unfortunately, there is no general answer to the sampling dilemma. The solution will often be specific to the community and the subgroup of interest. The best advice seems to be to work with a variety of community groups and leaders to attempt to construct as complete a list of potential participants as possible, and then to randomly sample from that list.

Planning for Successful Focus Group Interviews. Particularly when working with particular subgroups of the community population, several steps can be taken to increase the level and quality of participation in the focus groups. For example, enlisting the support of a respected neighborhood or community leader to request citizen participation can be very useful. The focus group coordinator should find a neutral and convenient location where citizens will feel comfortable expressing their opinion about the law enforcement agency. The focus group moderator/facilitator should be sensitive to cultural and language differences and possible distrust of the police. Further, it is the responsibility of the moderator to ensure that the environment of the focus group setting is nonthreatening and nonjudgmental so that participants feel free to express their opinions.

Conclusion

Citizen surveys and focus groups serve multiple purposes for law enforcement. Through WSICOP's work with a number of agencies, we have seen the results of the surveys and focus groups used in a variety of ways. These have included presentations to city and county councils on the agency's performance and on the public's call for more police resources. Many agencies use the results in internal planning efforts to address specific neighborhood problems. In another community, the results led to efforts to recruit members of minority groups to the citizen's academy. In several communities, tangible outcomes such as the opening of a neighborhood mini-station or the deployment of bicycle patrols have resulted. Whatever the use of the findings, however, the important lesson is that if the police-community partnership is to truly be a partnership, law enforcement needs to develop ways to listen to this partner. Surveys and focus groups are two key methods that can help agencies open such a dialogue.

References

Alpert, G., and M.H. Moore (1993). "Measuring Police Performance in a New Paradigm of Policing." In *Performance Measures for the Criminal Justice System*. Washington, DC: U.S. Government Printing Office.

Bureau of Justice Assistance (1993). *A Police Guide to Surveying Citizens and Their Environment*. Washington, DC: U.S. Government Printing Office.

Dillman, D.A. (1978). *Mail and Telephone Surveys: The Total Design Method*. New York, NY: John Wiley and Sons.

Pate, A.M., M.A. Wycoff, W.G. Skogan, and L.W. Sherman (1986). *Reducing Fear of Crime in Houston and Newark: A Summary Report*. Washington, DC: Police Foundation.

Problem-Solving Auto Theft in Unincorporated Hillsborough County, Florida 13

Carl W. Hawkins, Jr.
Hillsborough County Sheriff's Office

Introduction

Since 1985, a variety of strategies have been tried to reduce the problem of auto thefts in the unincorporated areas of Hillsborough County, Florida. For example, the Hillsborough County Sheriff's Office deployed street crime squads targeting areas where cars were reported stolen. An agency-wide task force also was implemented to combat auto theft. And auto theft detectives increased their efforts by focusing on auto salvage yards where motor vehicles were being chopped into parts. While each of these traditional methods succeeded to a limited extent, none proved to have a substantial and lasting impact.

Beginning in 1990, the explosion of the juvenile population in Florida fueled an increase in property crimes. In unincorporated Hillsborough County, juveniles targeted burglary, larceny, and auto theft for their criminal activities. Between 1990 and 1994, auto theft rose by 71 percent and unincorporated Hillsborough County rose to the rank of the second highest county in Florida for auto theft. Hillsborough County had achieved the largest increase and the greatest number of stolen motor vehicles ever reported in the county's nearly 150-year history.

Citizens also were becoming alarmed by the growing juvenile auto theft problem. They expressed their consternation to the sheriff's office through letters, phone calls, and community meetings. The media further magnified the issue by doing in-depth stories of 12 people who were killed in or by stolen motor vehicles. The community and the media urged the sheriff's office to find a solution to this problem.

Unincorporated Hillsborough County

Located on the gulf coast of Florida, unincorporated Hillsborough County is a large suburban/rural community with one of the largest cargo ports in the southeastern United States. With only three incorporated cities (Tampa, Temple Terrace, and Plant City), nearly two-thirds of the population and seven-eighths of the land mass occupy the unincorporated portion of the county. Suburban subdivisions with upscale neighborhoods and large tracts of agricultural land represent much of the land mass. Housing starts, tourism, and commodities such as strawberries, tomatoes, citrus, beef, poultry, and dairy represent the major economic fuel behind the population growth and economic development in unincorporated Hillsborough County.

Problem Solving

In 1989, the Hillsborough County Sheriff's Office contracted with the Police Executive Research Forum to teach problem solving to the command staff. Problem-solving training emphasized the SARA model and the crime triangle.

The SARA model is an analytical problem-solving tool developed by the Police Executive Research Forum with the assistance of the Newport News, Virginia, Police Department. SARA is an acronym that stands for scanning, analysis, response, and assessment. Teaching deputies the SARA approach provided them with a structured problem-solving methodology.

The crime triangle is based on the assumption that most crime is concentrated on repeat victims and offenders. For a crime to occur, the victim, offender, and location must intersect at some point in time. By strategically examining information on the victim, offender, and location, you can readily determine that there are guardians, controllers, and/or managers who exercise some control over each side of the crime triangle. Guardians, controllers, and/or managers provide responses that can influence one side of the triangle in a different manner and, therefore, affect the ability of the three sides to intersect at a given point in time. Without this intersection, crime is prevented.

From 1990 to 1993, supervisors, deputies, and new recruits were taught the SARA model and the crime triangle as part of a new training course. A standard operating procedure and a problem-analysis report were created to provide a way to document the problem-solving projects. A problem-analysis advisory committee also was developed to review the problem-solving projects. The committee also established a library for past projects. Deputies now had a place to go to review similar projects and strategies that may be useful in solving the problem they have encountered. Deputies now had a workable method for problem solving and could apply this process as part of their daily job.

Community Policing

In 1993, a community policing model that focused on the core components of community engagement and problem solving was developed. This model gave deputies ownership of specific community resource areas. The deputies identified 26 neighborhoods in unincorporated Hillsborough County where calls for service and problems were concentrated.

Each area had a community council that worked with a deputy on collaborative problem solving in their neighborhoods. A survey administered in the 26 community resource areas listed auto theft as one of the most serious problems facing each of these communities. The community councils were also concerned about the 12 people killed in or by stolen motor vehicles. The community resource deputies began working on the problem. Early recognition that this problem was widespread across the 26 community areas led to agreement that an agency-wide collaborative strategy was needed.

Drawing on the problem-solving experience of the sheriff's office, two agency-wide strategies were developed to reduce the number of auto thefts in unincorporated Hillsborough County. These were Operation "HEAT" (Help Eliminate Auto Theft) and "Training, Education, & Apprehension—A Three-Pronged Attack on Auto Theft." Each focused on reducing auto theft through the problem-solving process.

Operation HEAT (Help Eliminate Auto Theft)

In 1993, Operation HEAT (Help Eliminate Auto Theft) was initiated. The focus of this strategy was on education and public awareness of the problem of auto theft, measures to prevent victimization by motor vehicle theft, and emphasis on the consequences of being arrested for this crime. In unincorporated Hillsborough County, juveniles represented the largest group who were stealing motor vehicles.

To assist deputies in teaching the training classes, information was obtained on the types of locations where motor vehicles were stolen and what makes and models were most popular with thieves. This information also was printed on tri-fold handouts and distributed in the community resource areas that had experienced the largest number of thefts.

Motor vehicles were stolen from:

- driveways of single-family dwellings, or from apartment complex parking lots or parking garages (50%)

- parking lots or parking garages (36%)

- stores or shopping malls (8%)

- hotels or motels (3%)

- office buildings (2%)

- schools, universities, or nightclubs (1%)

Table 13.1
Vehicles Stolen Most Often

Make	Model
Chevrolet (20.6%)	Camaro (7.1%)
	Monte Carlo (3%)
	Caprice (2.4%)
	Celebrity (1.8%)
Pontiac (12%)	Forthcoming Grand Prix (4.1%)
	Trans Am (2.4%)
Oldsmobile (10.9%)	Cutlass (4.7%)
Ford (9.2%)	Pickup (3%)
Buick (8.7%)	Regal (4.7%)
Mazda (4.3%)	RX-7 (4.7%)
Cadillac (3.8%)	
Honda (3.8%)	Accord (2.4%)
Toyota (3.8%)	
Jeep (3.3%)	Cherokee (2.4%)
All Others (19.6%)	

Training classes were offered at community meetings (potential victims) on the problem of auto theft and ways to prevent motor vehicle thefts from occurring. Additional training classes were offered at the middle schools to educate youths (potential offenders) on the consequences of this crime. Steering wheel locking mechanisms also were given away during the training classes. Billboards, posters, displays, and tri-fold handouts in English and Spanish were made available in the target areas where the highest incidents of stolen motor vehicles were reported. A tip line also was established by the sheriff's office to report who was stealing the cars and where the thieves might be found.

Training, Education, & Apprehension—A Three-Pronged Attack on Auto Theft

In 1996, another strategy to reduce auto theft was implemented. The Training, Education, & Apprehension—A Three-Pronged Attack on Auto Theft program concentrated on a comprehensive, specialized auto theft training approach taught to deputies, detectives, other law enforcement agencies, and the State Attorney's Office. Additional educational programs were offered to citizens in the community resource areas where reported auto theft was high. Collaboration between the sheriff's office and the U.S. Customs, Tampa Port Authority, Seaboard Tampa Terminals, and CSX Transportation was instituted to apprehend those responsible for stealing motor vehicles in unincorporated Hillsborough County. This strategy expanded the efforts of Operation HEAT and additionally went after adult criminals, including drug users and professional thieves.

To help with this effort, the State Attorney's Office of Hillsborough County was trained in case preparation and successful prosecution of auto theft and related offenses. In addition, unannounced inspections of the cargo ports and railroad yards in Tampa were implemented to reduce an avenue of distribution for stolen motor vehicles bound for Central and South America, Asia, and to a lesser extent, U.S. territories.

Results

With the implementation of Operation HEAT (1993, 1994, 1995) and Training, Education, & Apprehension—A Three-Pronged Attack on Auto Theft (1996, 1997, 1998), auto thefts decreased by 68 percent, or 1,680 reported stolen motor vehicles, between 1994 and 1998. This represented the largest decrease in stolen automobiles in the past decade. Furthermore, a subsequent survey determined that auto theft was no longer a major problem in many of the 26 community resource areas.

Conclusion

Auto theft is a problem in many growing communities and regions across the United States. In unincorporated Hillsborough County, auto theft rose due to a dramatic increase in the juvenile population within an area that included a large cargo port and railroad yard for domestic and international trade. To reduce this problem, the collaborative efforts of education, apprehension, information sharing, and prosecution were used. The SARA model and the crime triangle approach, in combination with collaborative problem solving, helped to provide an effective strategy to reduce the problem of auto theft in both size and scope.

Despite the success mentioned above, the problem of auto theft in unincorporated Hillsborough County has not been completely eliminated. Furthermore, this problem might worsen again in the future. There are some indications the juvenile population may substantially increase within the next five years in unincorporated Hillsborough County. However, if this were to happen, established and workable collaborative efforts already are in place. Deputies, other agencies, and the State Attorney's Office have been trained. The community resource areas have experience in problem solving. Training programs and materials have been developed. Partnerships are in place with the U.S. Customs Office, the Tampa Port Authority, and domestic railroad yards. These collaborative efforts provide a field-tested response to future auto theft problems in unincorporated Hillsborough County.

A lesson learned from these efforts is the complex nature of auto theft. No one strategy will reduce the problem. Multiple collaborative partnerships must be formed. The key is to recognize that many tactics and methods must be consistently applied in neighborhoods and communities over time to reduce the incidence of auto theft.

Innovative Community Crime Prevention: An Overview of the Mountlake Terrace Neutral Zone-AmeriCorps Program 14

David G. Mueller
Boise State University

Quint C. Thurman
Southwest Texas State University

Cary Heck
Louisiana State University—Health Sciences Center

Introduction

Most criminologists agree that it is far better to prevent crime in the first place than to allow it to happen and then invoke a criminal justice system response to it. Even so, proponents of crime prevention may disagree about how best to keep crime from occurring (Jensen & Rojek, 1998). For example, some scholars have suggested that long-term incarceration is, in fact, one of the most effective forms of crime prevention (see Sherman, Gottfredson, Mackenzie, Eck, Reuter & Bushway, 1998). Requiring high-rate offenders to serve longer sentences, otherwise known as "selective incapacitation," is referred to as "secondary crime prevention." Such an approach is effective to the extent that it increases our capacity to reduce the likelihood of future offenses by those who already have proven themselves unable to abide by society's laws.

Primary crime prevention programs, on the other hand, differ from secondary prevention efforts in that they try to prevent crime proactively by changing deviant values, undesirable habits, and subcultural processes thought to be linked with antisocial behavior. That is, rather than attempting to control repeat offenders after they have been socialized into criminal lifestyles, primary prevention efforts are designed to set them out on a different path altogether.

In most cases, primary prevention efforts are targeted at youths. One reason for this is that school-aged children are an accessible audience who are assumed to be receptive to anti-delinquency messages. Youths also are a good target group for another reason. A sizeable proportion of today's delinquents are expected to become tomorrow's criminals offenders (Visher, 2000; Wolfgang, Figlio & Sellin, 1972).

There is a wide variety of primary prevention programs in operation today (see Gottfredson, 1997); the most well-known of these is DARE. DARE is an example of primary prevention because it seeks to prevent adolescent deviance by teaching kids to avoid behaviors such as drug use and delinquency. However, recent studies of DARE programs indicate that, despite its obvious popularity among parents, teachers, and police officers, DARE has yielded neither significant short-term nor long-term reductions in adolescent drug use (cf., Ennett, Tobler, Ringwalt & Flewelling, 1994; Rosenbaum, Flewelling, Bailey, Ringwalt & Wilkinson, 1994; Wysong, Aniskiewicz & Wright, 1994). In a nutshell, these studies all point up the fact that "a few hours of classroom instruction has little chance of altering a lifetime of learning from parents, peers, and the larger community" (Weisheit, 1983:74).

Perhaps it is unfair to single out DARE for its obvious shortcomings without mentioning that a wide variety of well-established, school-based prevention programs (e.g., sex education and driver's education) appear to have had little positive impact on potentially dangerous adolescent behavior (see Brokowski & Baker, 1974; Hackler, 1978; Smith & Gorry, 1980). "Indeed, the majority of community-based [prevention] programs may fall victim to a common criticism—they sound good, feel good, look good, but do not work good" (Fritsch, Caeti & Taylor, 1999:127).

A notable exception to this apparent pattern of failed primary crime prevention programs is an innovative, yet little-known, delinquency prevention program currently operating in western Washington called the Neutral Zone. The Neutral Zone was developed by former Mountlake Terrace Police Chief John Turner, who, in the early 1990s, was under considerable public pressure to "do something" to reduce the growing threat of serious juvenile crime.

Background

The city of Mountlake Terrace, Washington, is a working-class suburb located several miles north of Seattle. Like other cities located near a large urban center, Mountlake Terrace has had its share of crime and disorder, but in the early 1990s city officials were struggling to cope with what appeared to be an unprecedented surge of serious juvenile crime. For example, in the five-year period between 1988 and 1992, juvenile arrests within the city of Mountlake Terrace rose by an alarming 63 percent. Additionally, the rate of juvenile arrests for violent crimes statewide had virtually doubled since 1982, even though there were fewer juveniles in the 10- to 17-year-old at-risk age group (GJJAC, 1992).

Mountlake Terrace's juvenile crime problems came to a head during the summer of 1990. On back-to-back weekends in August 1990, Mountlake Terrace firefighters responded to a rash of suspicious fires that destroyed several prominent businesses and private dwellings in and around the city's commercial district. As residents arrived to watch the fires rage in the wee hours of the morning, it was hard for them not to notice the large number of juveniles who also had gathered at the scene. What were so many kids doing out at two o'clock in the morning, anyway? Shouldn't they be home at this hour? Surely they were up to no good. And thus the speculation began: kids had probably started the fires. Though the evidence linking juveniles to the fires was circumstantial (and in time turned out to be totally false), the recent rise in juvenile-related crime helped to reinforce what community residents already "knew." Something had to be done!

Instead of overreacting to the problem by jumping on the "curfew bandwagon," Chief Turner decided that the first order of business was to hold a series of public meetings to allow residents to vent their frustrations and to explore alternative solutions. As expected, most residents initially clamored for a citywide curfew. However, others disagreed, arguing that a curfew would deal only with the symptoms of juvenile crime rather than the reasons that it occurred in the first place. What was needed was a more permanent, proactive, and if possible, non-punitive solution.

Over time, the idea took hold that perhaps a better way to control juvenile delinquency would be to involve youths in a sports-related program in order to keep them busy and off the streets on weekend nights, when problems seemed to be at their worst. But would a "midnight basketball program" really produce the outcomes that local residents were hoping for? After reviewing a number of alternative strategies in various cities around the nation, Turner and a group of concerned Mountlake Terrace stakeholders called the Community Action Resource Team (CART) established a collaborative, nontraditional crime prevention program called the Neutral Zone. As originally designed, the Neutral Zone was created to: (1) reduce the likelihood of youth involvement in, as victims or perpetrators, crime or violence on Mountlake Terrace streets, specifically during the most active periods of the week; (2) make inroads into the city's youth culture in order to help prevent delinquent activity; (3) provide an arena where recreation and community services are available to high-risk youth during the most crucial hours; and (4) allow youth, community volunteers, police, and other helping professionals to work together in an effort to seek more positive outcomes for high-risk youth (CART, 1993).

Designed and implemented as a proactive, community-based response to the problem of youth crime, the Neutral Zone offers juvenile participants, ages 13 to 20, an alternative environment in which to more productively pass their time during the most crime-prone hours of the weekend on Fridays and Saturdays from 10:00 P.M. to 2:00 A.M. (see Payton, 1977; Levine & McEwen, 1985). It eventually evolved into a multifaceted, educational and service-oriented outreach program that substantially reduced juvenile crime in and around the Mountlake Terrace area (see Thurman, Giacomazzi, Reisig & Mueller, 1996; Thurman, Burton, Mueller & Heck, 1996).

Program Modifications

Although the Neutral Zone program was originally conceived as a safe haven for street kids and an alternative for wannabe gang members, it grew to include a wider range of prosocial activities. For example, in addition to its late-night recreational component, the program also offered youths both hot and cold meals during regular operating hours. As the number of participants grew, Neutral Zone staff and volunteers became aware that a number of the youths were in need of more regularized food and clothing services. Thus, charitable donations were solicited from private citizens and local businesses in order to establish a small food and clothing bank for the city's homeless and/or "throw away" kids. Interestingly, this service, which was primarily intended to help area youths, also appears to have benefited local merchants and the police department in unexpected ways. For example, by reducing the motivation for kids to steal food and clothing out of need, the food and clothing bank was helpful in reducing the number of petty crimes in the area, such as shoplifting and theft from local merchants.

While not designed as a cure-all for the many problems that youths face during their teenage years, the Neutral Zone also began to offer a number of health-related programs designed to benefit adolescents, including Alcoholics Anonymous, Narcotics Anonymous, HIV/AIDS awareness, smoking cessation, and CPR/first aid training. Other outside agencies, including Planned Parenthood and Pathways to Women, also offer program participants a number of social service seminars on topics such as birth control, anger management, assertiveness training, and other counseling services.

Functioning as an outreach program, the Neutral Zone also serves as a valuable source of police intelligence on crimes committed by (and against) area street youths. Working to establish ties between street youths and the police, the program also makes it easier for the police to influence juvenile behavior. And, while it is difficult to know with certainty what the long-term benefits of the Neutral Zone will be on kids, the police, and the community, responses from all parties over the past several years have been extremely positive (see Thurman, Burton, Mueller & Heck, 1996).

Evaluation Results

Chief Turner, a strong proponent of community policing, anticipated several positive outcomes for his community by taking the preventive route over a more reactive one. First, he worked from the assumption that youth would be attracted to a place that offered them interesting and engaging opportunities to participate in productive activities. Even so, the Neutral Zone fits the notion of "voluntary incarceration." That is, if the program could lure area youth into a supportive and controlled environment where activities and supervision could be effectively monitored, it might also help to cut down on the number of opportunities for youth to become either perpetrators or victims of criminal violence. In short, by involving area youth in structured, prosocial activities, the Neutral Zone made it possible to reduce the rates of both juvenile crime and victimization by simply offering the targeted group a more productive way to spend their free time.

An evaluation of the Neutral Zone in 1994 documented that approximately 150 to 200 youths attended the program each weekend night (Thurman, Giacomazzi & Reisig, 1994). Subsequent investigation of the program found that when the Neutral Zone was closed for repairs in the last week of July and the first week of August, 1994, police calls for service in the city increased almost 30 percent (Thurman, Giacomazzi, Reisig & Mueller, 1996:290). Additionally, a story that ran in the *Seattle Times* (Monday, April 8, 1996:A1) reported that graffiti in and around the Mountlake Terrace area had dropped from 85 incidents in 1994 to 28 in 1995, and gang-related crimes also dropped from 135 incidents to 93 during the same period.

Finally, a 1996 performance audit of an expanded version of the Neutral Zone found that it was making significant strides toward increasing its overall impact on area youth. For example, the addition of program services ranging from tutoring and homework assistance to mentoring classes for seventh- and eighth-grade latchkey youths not only appears to be keeping them busy but seems to be making a real contribution in terms of preparing these individuals for life after adolescence (Thurman, Burton, Mueller & Heck, 1996).

Discussion

Two problems that typically threaten innovations such as the Neutral Zone are maintaining program interest and maintaining adequate funding. For example, Oettmeier and Brown (1988:131-132) argue that the term "program" suggests a short-term commitment to a complex problem. Moreover, the term implies a need for a continuity in administrative leadership to ensure consistent priorities, clients, and stakeholders. Without such consistency, Oettmeier and Brown argue that program participants (as well as staff and volunteers) soon get the message that their input is not valued, and they eventually lose interest. Neutral Zone administrators seemed to understand the nature of this process and worked diligently to maintain their commitment to program goals. Funding has been a second major challenge.

In order to cut down on initial startup costs of the program, Chief Turner and CART opted to locate the program in a local elementary school in a residential area of the city. Although the building itself could be used free of charge, concerns were raised about possible litigation costs that might be incurred if someone was hurt while attending the program. To ward off this possibility, Chief Turner and CART successfully petitioned state legislators to change the wording of existing laws to expand liability insurance to cover program participants.

While the Neutral Zone originally was supported by charitable donations from individual and corporate sponsors, as the program grew and the newness wore off, the Neutral Zone was faced with the need to cultivate greater and more longer-term sources of funding. Although fund-raising efforts proved relatively successful, program administrators soon learned that alternative sources of funding at both the state and local levels were not available except for the more punitive suppression tactics that simply did not fit with the program's ultimate goal of primary prevention or community interests.

In a move designed to distance themselves from the increasingly unpopular labels of "midnight basketball program" and "gang magnet," and at the same time obtain money for the program's survival, Neutral Zone administrators applied for funding through the recently enacted AmeriCorps program. At the time, Ameri-Corps was a relatively new and innovative program implemented under the National Service Act and signed into law by President Clinton in September 1993. Seeing this as an opportunity to expand their present services and capabilities, especially in the area of education and community service, the Neutral Zone was awarded a $236,000 grant to continue its operations in January 1995. New funding helped to support five AmeriCorps team leaders and 30 part-time assistants, although the core program itself continued to operate on a $150,000 budget with funds provided primarily from regional corporate sponsors such as the Boeing Corporation, Safeco, and the Paul Allen Foundation.

Beyond simple arrest statistics, the expanded Neutral Zone-AmeriCorps program continues to meet or exceed its stated goals. Additionally, the program seems to have promoted a solid connection between high-risk youths and their community. In this vein, Braithwaite (1989) argues that a connection of this type provides youths with the necessary foundations to make healthy life choices and to aid in the development of conventional life skills. Such an approach for the reduction of deviant behavior has been successful in providing a better and safer environment for both high-risk youths and the entire Mountlake Terrace community. Program participants and volunteers alike appear to glean a number of useful skills (e.g., education, job skill training, anger management, assertiveness training, etc.) that are assumed, in the long run, to make an important difference in the lives of troubled teenagers. Prompted in large part by Chief Turner's vision, the program has become an excellent example of police-community problem solving. And beyond that, the adaptability and persistence of the Neutral Zone has sowed the seeds for its continued success, despite the usual problems that eventually wear such programs down.

Conclusion

Juvenile delinquency and youth crime are both complex social issues. In combination they have the potential to outpace limited police resources while further straining community relations between teachers, parents, businesses, and public service agencies. However, as the Neutral Zone story suggests, these types of problems can be addressed and the damage reduced if both law enforcement and community members are willing to work cooperatively. The early success of the Neutral Zone can be attributed to the collaborative and community-based nature of the program. However, its continued success will likely depend upon its ability to adapt and to meet the changing needs of its clientele. Many rural and suburban communities are in a particularly suitable position to implement similar interventions. Given the persistent nature of juvenile delinquency and the apparent need for proactive law enforcement, community-building ventures such as the one described here offer promising solutions for challenging crime problems. However, as the term implies, "community building" must be a community effort. Toward that end, the Neutral Zone can serve as a model by which other jurisdictions can create their own police-community problem-solving teams.

References

Braithwaite, J. (1989). *Crime, Shame, and Reintegration*. Cambridge University Press.

Brokowski, A., and F. Baker (1974). "Professional, Organizational, and Social Barriers to Primary Prevention." *American Journal of Orthopsychiatry* 44 (5):707-719.

Community Action Resource Team (1993, November). *The Neutral Zone: A Non-Traditional Gang/Crime Prevention, Late Night Program for High Risk Kids*. Mountlake Terrace, WA: Mountlake Terrace Police Department.

Ennett, S., N. Tobler, C. Ringwalt, and R. Flewelling (1994). "How Effective is Drug Abuse Resistance Education? A Meta-Analysis of Project DARE Outcome Evaluations." *American Journal of Public Health* 84:1394-1401.

Fritsch, E., T. Caeti, and R. Taylor (1999). "Gang Suppression Through Saturation Patrol, Aggressive Curfew, and Truancy Enforcement: A Quasi-Experimental Test of the Dallas Anti-Gang Initiative." *Crime & Delinquency* 45:122-139.

Gottfredson, D.C. (1997). "School-Based Crime Prevention." In L.W. Sherman, D. Gottfredson, D. MacKenzie, J. Eck, P. Reuter, and S. Bushway (eds.), *Preventing Crime: What Works, What Doesn't, What's Promising: A Report to the United States Congress*. Washington, DC: U.S. Department of Justice (NCJ 165366).

Governor's Juvenile Justice Advisory Committee (1992). *Juvenile Justice Report*. Olympia, WA: Department of Social and Health Services.

Hackler, J. (1978). *The Prevention of Youthful Crime: The Great Stumble Forward*. Toronto: Methuen Press.

Jensen, G.F., and D.G. Rojek (1998) *Delinquency and Youth Crime,* Third Edition. Prospect Heights, IL: Waveland Press, Inc.

Oettmeier, T., and L.P. Brown (1988). "Developing a Neighborhood-Oriented Policing Style." In J.R. Green and S. Mastrofski (eds.), *Community Policing: Rhetoric or Reality?* New York, NY: Praeger.

Levine, M.J., and J.T. McEwen (1985). *Patrol Deployment*. Washington, DC: National Institute of Justice Report #J-LEAA-011-81.

Payton, G.T. (1977). *Patrol Procedure*. Los Angeles, CA: Legal Books Corporation.

Rosenbaum, D., R. Flewelling, S. Bailey, C. Ringwalt, and D. Wilkinson (1994). "Cops in the Classroom: A Longitudinal Evaluation of Drug Abuse Resistance Education (DARE)." *Journal of Research in Crime and Delinquency* 31:3-31.

Sherman, L.W., D.C. Gottfredson, D.L. MacKenzie, J. Eck, P. Reuter, and S.D. Bushway (1998, July). "Preventing Crime: What Works, What Doesn't, What's Promising." *National Institute of Justice Research in Brief*. Washington, DC: U.S. Department of Justice.

Smith, P., and G. Gorry (1980). "Evaluating Sex Education Programs." *Journal of Sex Education and Therapy* 6 (2):17-23.

Thurman, Q.C., V.S. Burton Jr., D.G. Mueller, and C. Heck (1996). *A Performance Audit of the Neutral Zone-Americorps Peer Assistance and Development Program*. Pullman, WA: Northwest Evaluation Research Institute.

Thurman, Q.C., A.L. Giacomazzi, and M.D. Reisig (1994). *A Process Evaluation of the Mountlake Terrace Neutral Zone Gang Intervention Program*. Spokane, WA: Washington State Institute for Community Oriented Policing.

Thurman, Q.C., A.L. Giacomazzi, M.D. Reisig, and D.G. Mueller (1996). "Community-Based Gang Prevention and Intervention: An Evaluation of The Neutral Zone." *Crime & Delinquency* 42: 279-295.

Visher, C. (2000). "Career Criminals and Crime Control." In J. Sheley (ed.), *Criminology*, Fifth Edition. Belmont, CA: Wadsworth.

Weisheit, R. (1983). "The Social Context of Alcohol and Drug Education: Implications for Program Evaluations." *Journal of Alcohol and Drug Education* 29:72-81.

Wolfgang, M., R.M. Figlio, and T. Sellin (1972). *Delinquency in a Birth Cohort*. Chicago, IL: University of Chicago Press.

Wysong, E., R. Aniskiewicz, and D. Wright (1994). "Truth and DARE: Tracking Drug Education to Graduation and as Symbolic Politics." *Social Problems* 41:448-473.

Section IV
Rural Community Policing and the Future

Future Challenges: The Urbanization of Rural America

Ralph A. Weisheit
Illinois State University

Steven T. Kernes
Federal Law Enforcement Training Center

Introduction

Predicting the future is a notoriously risky venture, but it is a useful one. Good management and leadership require planning and preparation. Unfortunately, far too often "vision" extends no further than the next budget cycle. Given the limited resources with which they work, planning for the future is particularly important for small-town and rural police executives. Successful rural and small-town police administrators must conceptualize, have a vision of the twenty-first century, develop goals and plans predicated on this vision, and take appropriate actions to implement their plans.

While we have no perfect vision of the future, we can make projections based on current trends. Anticipating and understanding future changes in rural America, and the implications of those changes for rural crime and rural policing requires an appreciation for the variations in rural areas. Rural areas cover a wide spectrum, but for this discussion we will simplify reality by considering two extreme categories of rural. At the one extreme is a rural America steeped in poverty and high unemployment, with few prospects for a brighter future. This rural America is often physically and socially distant from urban centers. At the other extreme is a rural America that is relatively prosperous, is experiencing population growth, and for which the future is brightest. This rural America is often, though not always, within reach of large cities.

While many forces shaping our future might be included (see Weisheit & Donnermeyer, 2000), the discussion that follows focuses on three particular issues and their implications for rural crime and rural policing. These issues are population, the economy, and technology.

Key Issues

Population

For much of its early history, the United States was an agrarian society in which most citizens lived in rural areas. In 1790, for example, there were only eight communities in the United States with more than 5,000 people, and the entire population of the nation was less than four million people. By 1900, the U.S. population had risen to 76 million people, and by early 2001 the estimated population was more than 283 million people and was experiencing a net gain of one person every 17 seconds (U.S. Bureau of the Census, 1995:8; U.S. Bureau of the Census, 2001). It is projected that by 2025 there will be more than 338 million people in this country (U.S. Bureau of the Census, 1995:9).

What are the implications of this continued growth for rural America? Despite its rapid population growth, much of the United States lives outside of urban areas. In 1990, for example, nearly 70 percent of the counties in the United States had fewer than 50,000 people, and these nonmetropolitan counties contained about one-quarter of the population of the nation. Thus, while most people live in urban areas, most places in America are still rural. As of 1992, 87 percent of the incorporated communities in the United States had fewer than 10,000 people (U.S. Bureau of the Census, 1995:43). Although many of these communities are within the shadow of urban centers, the point remains that large city centers are the exception rather than the rule. Population growth will gradually reduce the amount of rural territory, but rural will continue to be a viable concept, and that is likely to be true for some time to come.

Continued population growth and urban sprawl will mean a steady reduction in the number of rural areas and a continuous supply of places in transition from rural to suburban or urban. "Across the nation, 1 million acres of farmland are being converted to urban or suburban uses each year, a rate of two acres per minute" (Brandon, 1996). In California's Central Valley, for example, it is estimated that by the year 2040 the population will triple and housing will use more than one million acres of irrigated farmland (Goldberg, 1996). However, population growth will not be evenly distributed across rural areas. Most growth will occur in rural areas adjacent to urban centers. While such growth will be a boon to the local economy, it also will lead to higher crime rates. Some have suggested that when small towns grow very rapidly, the crime rate may increase three to four times faster than the population (Freudenburg & Jones, 1991). Others have found that rural areas experiencing growth are more likely than other rural areas to report the presence of gangs and the migration of urban gang members (Wells & Weisheit, 2000; Weisheit & Wells, 2000). It is probably true that most community leaders are better prepared for economic growth than for a substantial increase in crime. It will be important that small-town and rural police be sensitive to rapid population increases and take them into account in their long-term planning.

The differences between relatively affluent and growing rural areas and rural areas that are impoverished will persist and will probably increase over time. Many of the most remote rural areas will continue to see an exodus of people, particularly of young people and skilled workers.

The population of the United States is not only growing in number, but it is aging as well. While people age 55 or over make up about 20 percent of the population, by the year 2025 they will comprise 25 percent of the population. The number of people 65 years and older is increasing by 2.4 percent annually. "By the year 2025 at the latest, the proportion of all Americans who are elderly will be the same as the proportion in Florida today. America, in effect, will become a nation of Floridas and then keep aging. By 2040, one in four Americans may be over sixty-five" (Peterson, 1996:15). By the year 2080 there will be more than 1 million centenarians in the United States (Beck, Chideya & Craffey, 1992).

In 1950, there were 16 workers for each Social Security recipient. By the year 2030 there will be two workers for every recipient, and by 2050 one worker will support one recipient (Hardy & Hardy, 1992). When the cost of Medicare is added to the cost of Social Security, the figures become staggering. "The combined federal cost of Social Security and Medicare, expressed as a share of workers' taxable payroll, is officially projected to rise from the already burdensome 17 percent in 1995 to between 35 and 55 percent in 2040" (Peterson, 1996:9).

The greying of America's population will also have an impact on rural America. Drawn by a lower cost of living, relatively less crime, and a slower pace of life, small towns and rural areas have been popular retirement locations. As the number of retirees continues to grow, the number who retire to rural areas will also grow. For rural and small-town police, large groups of senior citizens are a mixed blessing. On the one hand, the crime rate among senior citizens is very low and many senior citizens have relatively good financial resources. On the other hand, their calls for service can be high and these calls are often for relatively minor problems. While the objective risk of victimization for senior citizens is low, their fear of crime is often high and they will expect local police to be sensitive to their concerns and to be responsive when they call. Because of their concerns about crime, senior citizens are best served by a highly visible police force that interacts frequently with citizens, precisely the style encouraged by community policing.

Senior citizens can also be excellent community partners, working with the police as watchful citizens. They may also provide a pool of volunteers to assist local police. Thoughtful police administrators will seek out ways to most effectively work with their senior citizens and to utilize them as a valuable community resource.

The Economy

For many people, rural is still synonymous with an agricultural economy. While this may have been true at one time, today only about 10 percent of rural residents work in agriculture. Other extraction industries, such as logging and mining, have also seen sharp declines in employment. Technological advances have dramatically reduced the number of jobs in these extraction industries, and this is particularly true for agriculture (Johnson, 1990). Today's rural economies are more likely to depend on state and local government jobs, service occupations, and recreation.

In the future, it is likely that local, state, and federal governments will continue to limit increases in spending. In the past, government employment had a major economic impact on rural areas, particularly the more remote rural areas. In the future, economic growth from government jobs will likely be limited—with an important exception. Because most prisons are located in rural areas, the increasing use of imprisonment as a punishment will disproportionately affect rural areas. For example, between 1980 and 1990, five percent of the increase in the rural population was accounted for by an influx of prison inmates (Beale, 1993), and there are now more prison inmates in the United States than there are farmers. For the near future, at least, it is likely that government spending and employment in corrections will continue to increase rapidly, and this will affect employment and the economies of rural areas. Unfortunately, expenditures on prison may provide employment in the host community, but it does little to foster long-term economic development of the area (Moberg, 1996). Thus, it is a poor instrument for economic growth.

The poorest rural communities will also be hard hit by continuing restrictions on public assistance. In these areas, the low skill level of the population and the remoteness of the area make it difficult to attract industry. Public aid is often a substantial portion of the local economy. Consider the following description of Owsley County, Kentucky (Jouzaitis, 1996):

> . . . in Owsley County (population 5,000), the annual per capita income is $5,791, a fraction of the national average of about $21,000 . . . Some 60 percent of Owsley's children live in poverty and half the adult population has less than a ninth-grade education.

The problem is compounded by the practice of building subsidized housing in rural areas and encouraging the urban poor to move there. As public aid expenditures continue to shrink, those with marketable skills will continue to exit, leaving the elderly and unskilled. What will remain will be a small tax base with which to fund police services.

Rural communities can expect substantial growth from service industries, particularly those drawing on emerging technologies. For example, companies that provide services through telephones, computer bulletin boards, or the Internet can just as easily locate in rural communities as in cities. The rise of satellite communi-

cations has opened rural areas to many occupations that, in the past, were techno-
logically practical only in large cities. These companies will be drawn to rural areas
by the lifestyle and by lower taxes, less crime, and lower wages. "Smaller places
are particularly likely to attract functions that require relatively lower skills and a
high percentage of clerical workers (such as telemarketing), that must keep operating costs to a minimum, and that have limited needs for travel and for other services" (Atkinson, 1996:42).

Advances in communications and technology will bring not only companies
to rural areas, but individual workers as well. Montana has already seen an influx
of "modem cowboys" (McDonald, 1996; Margolis, 1993; Wilkinson, 1996):

> . . . here the modem cowboys are gathering, telecommunicating their way to work,
> gaining economic and political influence, transforming Montana's traditional cul-
> ture and making enemies along the way. They are the industrial engineers, the
> shopping-center planners, the software designers and others who can live and
> work anyplace reached by fiber-optic cables. Not surprisingly, many of them want
> to live and work amid the cattle, elk, tall timber and rushing rivers so plentiful in
> Montana.

> . . . Because there are only about 800,000 Montanans, Montana could become the
> first state whose political and social culture is determined by this new breed of
> free-wheeling, independent-minded professional (Margolis, 1993).

This trend will not only be fueled by the technology that makes it possible, but
also by rising gasoline prices, which makes commuting expensive, and by concerns
about urban congestion and pollution, which leads many employers to encourage
telecommuting. And, while the Montana example may be the most colorful, a
greater impact is likely to be seen among rural areas adjacent to large cities. From
these areas workers will be able to do much of their work at home, periodically
visiting the office in town.

The movement of work from a central location to the home will also raise a
host of liability issues. Who is responsible if the employee is injured at home "on
company time?" Asset management, theft, and misappropriation or misuse of
company property will become serious issues. One response of companies will be
to increase the use of these "distance workers" as consultants or contract employees.

A growing number of rural communities have come to rely on tourism and
recreation for their economic base (Usdansky, 1994; Sneider, 1996; Nasser &
Overberg, 1996), and this trend will likely continue for some time. Tourism brings
its own set of crime problems, particularly given the high volume of people who are
in the area for only a short while. Rural police administrators in these communities
will face special challenges. For example, how does one maintain a viable year-
round police force for a community that may have as few as 5,000 permanent
residents, but whose population during the tourist season may swell to 70,000
people?

In the 1980s and 1990s, the lack of legitimate economic activities led some rural citizens to cultivate marijuana and assist in the transshipment of drugs across the United States. There has also been evidence that the remoteness of rural areas has made them appealing to methamphetamine lab operators, because these labs often produce noxious odors that are difficult to conceal in more densely populated areas (National Institute of Justice, 1993). Future projections are that methamphetamine use will increase, both in the United States and around the world. If that is true, a simultaneous increase in rural drug labs can be expected. It is possible that remote rural areas will become key producers of the marijuana and methamphetamines consumed in urban, suburban, and rural areas.

Finally, economic problems and disrupted job markets in rural America appear to have played a role in the rise of antigovernment groups in the 1980s and 1990s (Corcoran, 1990; Davidson, 1990; Coates, 1987; Flynn & Gerhardt, 1989). Many, perhaps most, of these groups have operated out of rural areas (Weisheit, Falcone & Wells, 1999). Some of these groups have done little more than talk about their concerns, while a small number have become involved in violence aimed at government officials, racial minorities, and Jews. The conditions that gave rise to these groups have not gone away, and some are predicting another farm crisis that would further fuel these extremist groups (Dyer, 1996). Rural police must not only be prepared to deal with these groups, but must recognize that police are seen by these groups as an arm of the government and therefore an arm of the "enemy camp." While the strongest animosity is reserved for federal and state police, local police can easily become targets if they are willing to hold group members accountable for violating the law. Antigovernment extremist groups are less likely to thrive in the prosperous and rapidly growing rural areas adjacent to large cities. Rather, they are more likely to thrive in the economically stagnant rural areas, places in which police departments are most understaffed and have the fewest resources with which to work.

Technology

Technology has radically transformed rural life and will continue to bring change to rural areas. The rise of satellite communications has brought news and entertainment to even the most remote areas. The number of cellular telephone subscribers jumped from zero in 1983 to more than 24 million by 1994 (U.S. Bureau of the Census, 1995:575). Satellite dishes now dot the countryside, and in the near future these dishes will allow for connections to the Internet.

Technology will also play an important role in crime and crime prevention in rural areas. For example, the technology for tagging grain and livestock will continue to improve, making it easier to locate stolen agricultural products. Advanced communications technology, including access to the Internet, will also make it easier to draw rural residents into scams in which they are defrauded.

Farmers have already begun using navigation satellites to determine precise locations for planting and fertilizing, and this Global Positioning System technology will eventually be used by rural police in a variety of ways. Some of these applications include locating officers in need of backup and assistance and helping emergency vehicles locate the scene of an accident.

Alaska, easily the state with the largest rural land area, is already using interactive live video connections to conduct court business without requiring the judge or the accused to travel to a common site. The use of this technology to bring criminal justice to remote rural areas will expand. As the price of this technology drops and its quality increases, video justice will be increasingly appealing to rural states that need to contain costs.

In most rural areas, patrol and highway functions are a particularly important part of rural police work. This is partly because there are nearly four times as many road miles in rural areas as in urban areas (U.S. Bureau of the Census, 1995:627), and this large difference is expected to persist. Thus, changes in the design and operation of automobiles will have direct implications for rural police. In the not-too-distant future, there will be no gauges. Heads-Up Displays (HUD) will project instrument readings so they appear to float on the hood. Included will be a collision avoidance system, with front and rear radar units, and an on-board video screen displaying road conditions and vital features of surrounding terrain. Driving radar will illuminate the highway. Traction-control systems will prevent the vehicle's wheels from spinning and prevent brakes from locking during panic stops. A rapidly deployable airbag restraint system in the prisoner compartment will control violent outbursts when transporting suspects and prisoners. An electronic sensor will be installed in each patrol car to shut down the electronic system of vehicles fleeing the police. This will eliminate high-speed pursuits and reduce related injuries and deaths.

Major interstates and highways in economically prosperous rural areas will utilize the Autoguide system, which is currently being tested in Germany. This system will direct cars to their destination over the safest, fastest routes. Sensors in the roadway will monitor the traffic flow and relay information about delays or hazards to a computerized control center, which in turn will beam the data to computers on board the automobile. These systems are unlikely to be installed in the most rural areas. Consider Vermont, for example. In 1996 there were more miles of dirt roads than paved roads (8,000 miles versus 6,000 miles), and many citizens of Vermont actively lobby to prevent more roads from being paved (Rimer, 1996). Further, in many of the more remote rural areas the tax base is too small to pave or to maintain existing roads, let alone turn them into "smart" highways.

One of the biggest changes in technology for rural police will be developments in police radio communications. The current system is relatively primitive, and there are rural areas where deep valleys and high mountains block police radio signals. Presently, city, county, and state police often have difficulty talking to one another because mobile and handheld radios, according to manufacturers, can only be produced by band and/or frequency span. In the future, satellites will replace radio repeaters and increase reception to 100 percent geographical coverage and 100 percent reliability. Leading police radio manufacturers will finally use existing communications technology. A single police radio spanning multiple bands, 800 trunking, VHF, and UHF C will be developed by the year 2005. Overnight, this new technology will end more than 50 years of antiquated communications and create an optimum system enabling all law enforcement officers, cars, and agencies to communicate by selecting the desired frequency or band. Existing police radios will be obsolete. Police radios will no longer be housed in police cars. Technology will allow officers to carry their radios on their person, just as one might carry a cellular phone.

Although these technological advances will revolutionize police communications, this technology will first be found in the relatively prosperous rural areas adjacent to cities. It will be a much longer time before this technology is available to police in the more remote and economically depressed rural areas. For example, there are rural departments that cannot afford the basic fee to connect to their state system for license and criminal history checks. There are also departments in which officers must provide their own health insurance and even their own patrol cars. Such departments are in the minority, but they illustrate the desperate economic plight of some rural areas—a situation that will keep much new technology out of their reach.

Technology will also be used to address the problem of getting training to rural police. Currently, rural police often have difficulty going to training programs. Aside from the cost and the distance to training, departments with fewer than 10 officers (about half of the departments in the United States) find that sending an officer away for a week or two of training can be a hardship for the remaining officers, who must cover his or her shift. The same technology that higher education is using for distance learning and the establishment of "virtual universities" will be useful for delivering training to rural police. Training will be taken to rural departments and will be delivered at times most convenient for the officers.

Discussion

Changes in the population, the economy, and technology will bring about important changes in rural crime and rural policing in the future, but these changes will not affect all of rural America in the same way. In particular, the most isolated and economically depressed rural areas will continue to see little or no population growth. They will not experience much economic growth, and advances in technology will largely pass by police in these communities. In contrast, rural areas adjacent to metropolitan centers will see continued population growth and economic vitality. Police in these departments will have a younger and better-educated population from which to draw recruits to the department, and a tax base that will keep these officers well equipped with the latest that technology has to offer.

To summarize the major points made in this chapter, we return to the three major areas on which the discussion was based: population, the economy, and technology:

Population:

- Rural will continue as a viable concept.

- Areas adjacent to urban centers will continue to experience growth from urban sprawl.

- Remote rural areas will continue to see little population growth, or even a population decline.

- The aging of the population will have a particularly marked effect on rural areas, many of which are attracting senior citizens.

Economy:

- There will be little growth in communities that rely on public sector spending.

- Recreation will continue to be a rural growth industry.

- There will be continued growth in service industries.

- Extraction industries will continue to see declining employment.

- The rise of telecommuting will bring more professionals into rural areas.

- The problem of drug production in rural areas will increase, particularly the production of methamphetamines and marijuana.

- Rural police will have increasing problems with extremist groups.

Technology:

- The most remote rural areas will see the rise of live interactive "video justice."

- Technology will play an important role in rural crime prevention.

- Improvements in automobiles and highways will be particularly important for rural police.

- There will be dramatic improvements in police communications.

- Technology will play an important role in taking training to rural police.

Conclusion

America is likely to go through many changes in the future, and rural areas will be affected by these changes. It is important to remember, however, that some things will probably not change. Good communication skills and the ability to interact well with people have always been important in police work, and such skills have probably been even more important for rural police than for urban police (see Weisheit, Falcone & Wells, 1999). Whatever changes are brought about by technology, the economy, and the population, rural police in the future will still find that the most important asset they will have will be their ability to interact well and communicate effectively with their citizens. That is the essence of good policing and the essence of effective community policing.

References

Atkinson, R. (1996). "The Rise of the Information-Age Metropolis." *The Futurist* (July-August): 41-46.

Beale, C.L. (1993). "Prisons, Population, and Jobs in Nonmetro America." *Rural Development Perspectives* 8:16-19.

Beck, M., F. Chideya, and B. Craffey (1992). "Attention Willard Scott: More and More People Are Living to See 100." *Newsweek* (May 4): 75.

Brandon, K. (1996). "Suburbia Sprouts in California's Valley of Plenty." *The Chicago Tribune* (November 18): 1, 10.

Coates, J. (1987). *Armed and Dangerous: The Rise of the Survivalist Right*. New York, NY: Hill and Wang.

Corcoran, J. (1990). *Bitter Harvest: Gordon Kahl and the Posse Comitatus*. New York, NY: Penguin Books.

Davidson, O.G. (1990). *Broken Heartland: The Rise of America's Rural Ghetto*. New York, NY: The Free Press.

Dyer, J. (1996). "Ground Zero." *The Utne Reader* (November-December): 80-85, 116-118.

Flynn, K., and G. Gerhardt (1989). *The Silent Brotherhood: Inside America's Racist Underground*. New York, NY: The Free Press.

Freudenburg, W.R., and R.E. Jones (1991). "Criminal Behavior and Rapid Community Growth: Examining the Evidence." *Rural Sociology* 56:619-645.

Goldberg, C. (1996). "Alarm Bells Sounding as Suburbs Gobble Up California's Richest Farmland." *New York Times* June 20: A10.

Hardy, D.R., and C.C. Hardy (1992). *Social Insecurity*. New York, NY: Villard Books.

Johnson, D. (1990). "Population Decline in Rural America: A Product of Advances in Technology." *The New York Times* (September 11): A12.

Jouzaitis, C. (1996). "Still Poor, Appalachia Faces the New Welfare." *The Chicago Tribune* (November 11): 1, 14.

Margolis, J. (1993). "The Computer Cowboys." *The Chicago Tribune* (November 18): Section 2, p. 1.

McDonald, K. (1996). "Crowding the Country." *The Chronicle of Higher Education* (May 24): A7, A10.

Moberg, D. (1996). "State Jobs: Economic Boon or Bust?" *Illinois Issues* 22:14-23.

Nasser, H., and P. Overberg (1996). "Census Consensus: Less Dramatic Growth." *USA Today* (March 8): 6A.

National Institute of Justice (1993). *Controlling Chemicals Used to Make Illegal Drugs: The Chemical Action Task Force and the Domestic Chemical Action Group.* Washington, DC: U.S. Department of Justice.

Peterson, P.G. (1996). *Will America Grow Up Before It Grows Old?* New York, NY: Random House.

Rimer, S. (1996). "In Slow-Paced Vermont, the Dirt Road Reigns." *New York Times* (June 24): A1, A10.

Sneider, D. (1996). "In a Utah Town, It's Goodbye Miners, Hello Mountain Bikers." *The Christian Science Monitor* (November 1): 4.

Usdansky, M. (1994). "City Dwellers Find Green Acres Are Place to Be." *USA Today* (July 15): 8A.

U.S. Bureau of the Census (1995). *Statistical Abstract of the United States, 1995.* Washington, DC: U.S. Government Printing Office.

U.S. Bureau of the Census (2001). "POPClock Projection." [http://www.census.gov/main/popclock.html] (U.S. Census Bureau Internet site) (Accessed 2-1-01).

Weisheit, R.A., and J.F. Donnermeyer (2000). "Change and Continuity in Crime in Rural America." In *Criminal Justice 2000, Volume 1, The Nature of Crime: Continuity and Change.* (pp. 309-357). Washington, DC: The National Institute of Justice.

Weisheit, R.A., D.N. Falcone, and L.E. Wells (1999). *Crime and Policing in Rural and Small-Town America,* Second Edition. Prospect Heights, IL: Waveland Press, Inc.

Weisheit, R.A., and L.E. Wells (2000). "The Social Construction of Gangs in Nonmetropolitan Areas." Paper presented to the American Society of Criminology. San Francisco, CA.

Wells, L.E., and R.A. Weisheit (2000). "Gang Problems in Smaller Communities: A Longitudinal Assessment." Paper presented to the Academy of Criminal Justice Sciences. New Orleans, LA.

Wilkinson, T. (1996). "Rural Montana Rewrites Myth of Yuppie Sprawl." *The Christian Science Monitor* (October 10): 1, 4.

SPOKANE POLICE DEPARTMENT
EMPLOYEE SURVEY
1996

As a follow-up to the 1993 Spokane Police Department Employee Survey, the Criminal Justice Program at Washington State University-Spokane is conducting a study of changes that are taking place in the Department as it moves toward Community Oriented Policing. Faculty and senior graduate students will prepare periodic reports on evidence collected in this questionnaire to provide feedback to Spokane P.D. employees and command staff on efforts to promote planned changes in the Department.

This research instrument addresses topics such as job attachment, work satisfaction, work-based stress, opinions about police work, perceptions of the community, personal values, and feelings about how well the Department is being managed.

Your participation in this survey is completely VOLUNTARY; however, in order to gather representative information it is IMPORTANT that as many of you as possible respond to the survey. YOUR ANSWERS WILL BE KEPT COMPLETELY CONFIDENTIAL. They will be recorded so that no single individual can be identified. While your department will be provided with a report of research results, the information will be summarized to **ensure anonymity**. All survey material will be kept at W.S.U. in Pullman and will not be available to department officials. These provisions are designed to reassure you that your frank and honest views can be recorded without fear of violation of your anonymity.

The survey is divided into several sections. To ensure accurate information, please follow the instructions. Consider the questions carefully, and answer them as fairly and accurately as possible. Please use the postage-paid, pre-addressed envelope enclosed for your convenience.

THANK YOU FOR YOUR COOPERATION IN THIS IMPORTANT PROJECT.

SECTION ONE: These questions deal with aspects of your personal background and circumstances. This information is needed in order to allow the proper interpretation of results with respect to important groupings of employees (for example, recent hires versus 5-year police veterans, etc.)

1. Age: (Check one)
   ___ 24 or under
   ___ 25-29
   ___ 30-34
   ___ 35-39
   ___ 40-44
   ___ 45-49
   ___ 50+

2. Ethnicity: (Check one)
   ___ Asian-American
   ___ African-American
   ___ Caucasian/White
   ___ Mexican-American/Hispanic
   ___ Native American/Indian
   ___ Latino
   ___ Other

3. Gender: (Check one)
   ___ Male
   ___ Female

4. Please check the highest level of schooling you have completed:
   ___ Not a High School Graduate
   ___ High School Graduate (college degree not completed)
   ___ Some College (degree not completed)
   ___ Associate Degree
   ___ Bachelor's Degree
   ___ Some Graduate Coursework
   ___ Graduate degree
   ___ Other (please specify)_____

5. Are you a commissioned or non-commissioned employee?
   ___Commissioned   ___Non-Commissioned

6. Are you in a supervisory or non-supervisory position?
   ___Supervisory   ___   Non-supervisory

7. To what shift are you presently assigned? (Check one)
   ___Day Shift   ___Graveyard   ___Swing Shift   ___Other

8. FOR NON-COMMISSIONED EMPLOYEES—In which unit do you work? (Check one)
   ___Dispatch ___Records ___Administrative Services ___Other

9. FOR COMMISSIONED EMPLOYEES—What is your current rank? (Check one)
   ___Officer   ___Lieutenant
   ___Corporal   ___Captain, Asst. Chief, Chief
   ___Detective   ___Other _____
   ___Sergeant

10. How many years have you been employed by the Spokane Police Department?
    _____ years

11. How many years have you been employed in the criminal justice field?
    _____ years

12. People differ in their degree of commitment to the organizations in which they work. Some feel little attachment to their organizations, while others feel strong attachment to their place of work. How would you describe your feelings about the Spokane Police Department? (circle your response)

1	2	3	4	5	6	7	8
Slight Attachment			Moderate Attachment			Strong Attachment	Undecided

13. The following are some of the things people usually take into account in relation to their work. Please indicate the TWO that seem most desirable to you.

1st Choice   2nd Choice

_____ _____ 1. A good salary so that you do not have any worries about money.

_____ _____ 2. A safe job with no risk of unemployment.

_____ _____ 3. Working with people you like.

_____ _____ 4. Doing an important job that gives you a feeling of accomplishment.

14. There is a lot of talk these days about what your country's goals should be for the next 10 or 15 years. Listed below are some of the goals that different people say should be given top priority. Please indicate the one you yourself consider the most important in the long run. Please indicate your second choice as well.

1st Choice   2nd Choice

_____ _____ 1. Maintaining order in the nation.

_____ _____ 2. Giving the people more say in important government decisions.

_____ _____ 3. Fighting rising prices.

_____ _____ 4. Protecting freedom of speech.

SECTION TWO: This part of the questionnaire asks you to express your judgments about how you believe three different levels of management operate in the SPD— namely, first-line supervisors, middle managers (Lieutenants and Captains for commissioned ranks), and top management (Chief, Assistant Chief, and Deputy Chief).

There are no correct or incorrect answers here; we are interested in how you judge each of these questions in terms of your observations and experiences at work. Please circle the number [1=disagree and 10=agree] that best reflects your view.

1. This level of management clearly communicates the purpose and rationale behind new programs, activities, and responsibilities in a way that wins employee acceptance.

First-Line Supervisors
Disagree 1   2   3   4   5   6   7   8   9   10   Agree
Middle Management
Disagree 1   2   3   4   5   6   7   8   9   10   Agree
Top Management
Disagree 1   2   3   4   5   6   7   8   9   10   Agree

2. This level of administration actively works to communicate the agency's "vision" and mission to employees. Developing a shared vision and set of values is a fundamental objective of this agency's management.

First-Line Supervisors
Disagree 1   2   3   4   5   6   7   8   9   10   Agree
Middle Management
Disagree 1   2   3   4   5   6   7   8   9   10   Agree
Top Management
Disagree 1   2   3   4   5   6   7   8   9   10   Agree

3. Employees feel they can trust this level of management. They feel comfortable putting their fate in the hands of these managers.

First-Line Supervisors
Disagree 1   2   3   4   5   6   7   8   9   10   Agree
Middle Management
Disagree 1   2   3   4   5   6   7   8   9   10   Agree
Top Management
Disagree 1   2   3   4   5   6   7   8   9   10   Agree

4. When assigning projects and responsibilities, such as Community Oriented Policing initiatives, this level of management makes sure that employees have sufficient power and authority to accomplish agency objectives.

First-Line Supervisors
Disagree 1   2   3   4   5   6   7   8   9   10   Agree
Middle Management
Disagree 1   2   3   4   5   6   7   8   9   10   Agree
Top Management
Disagree 1   2   3   4   5   6   7   8   9   10   Agree

5. This level of management practices what it preaches in terms of management values, work effort, and reforms. Leaders set good examples for others to follow. Credibility between words and actions is high.

First-Line Supervisors
Disagree 1   2   3   4   5   6   7   8   9   10   Agree
Middle Management
Disagree 1   2   3   4   5   6   7   8   9   10   Agree
Top Management
Disagree 1   2   3   4   5   6   7   8   9   10   Agree

6. This level of administration follows through on its promises regarding changes and reforms it expects employees to carry out.

First-Line Supervisors
Disagree 1   2   3   4   5   6   7   8   9   10   Agree
Middle Management
Disagree 1   2   3   4   5   6   7   8   9   10   Agree
Top Management
Disagree 1   2   3   4   5   6   7   8   9   10   Agree

7. This level of management actively seeks to reward, praise, and recognize high performance. It expects extremely high productivity and will not tolerate mediocrity. Leaders let employees know when they are doing well.

First-Line Supervisors
Disagree 1   2   3   4   5   6   7   8   9   10   Agree
Middle Management
Disagree 1   2   3   4   5   6   7   8   9   10   Agree
Top Management
Disagree 1   2   3   4   5   6   7   8   9   10   Agree

8. When routines result in just average performance, this level of management looks for ways to alter the status quo, and actively initiates changes, such as in work procedures, programs, and responsibilities to make them more effective.

First-Line Supervisors
Disagree 1   2   3   4   5   6   7   8   9   10   Agree
Middle Management
Disagree 1   2   3   4   5   6   7   8   9   10   Agree
Top Management
Disagree 1   2   3   4   5   6   7   8   9   10   Agree

9. This level of management experiments—such as with new ideas, work procedures, or task responsibilities—and it learns from mistakes.

First-Line Supervisors
Disagree 1   2   3   4   5   6   7   8   9   10   Agree
Middle Management
Disagree 1   2   3   4   5   6   7   8   9   10   Agree
Top Management
Disagree 1   2   3   4   5   6   7   8   9   10   Agree

10. This level of management actively plans for the future, and has established a clear vision of the organization's future.

First-Line Supervisors
Disagree 1   2   3   4   5   6   7   8   9   10   Agree
Middle Management
Disagree 1   2   3   4   5   6   7   8   9   10   Agree
Top Management
Disagree 1   2   3   4   5   6   7   8   9   10   Agree

11. This level of management is sensitive to changes in its environment, and is skillful in responding and adapting to short-term demands and needs.

First-Line Supervisors
Disagree 1   2   3   4   5   6   7   8   9   10   Agree
Middle Management
Disagree 1   2   3   4   5   6   7   8   9   10   Agree
Top Management
Disagree 1   2   3   4   5   6   7   8   9   10   Agree

12. This level of management has a deep and frequent interest in reform and change. These leaders are always coming up with new ideas on how to do things better.

First-Line Supervisors
Disagree 1   2   3   4   5   6   7   8   9   10   Agree
Middle Management
Disagree 1   2   3   4   5   6   7   8   9   10   Agree
Top Management
Disagree 1   2   3   4   5   6   7   8   9   10   Agree

13. This level of management is willing to engage in some risks to bring about change and reform.

First-Line Supervisors
Disagree 1   2   3   4   5   6   7   8   9   10   Agree
Middle Management
Disagree 1   2   3   4   5   6   7   8   9   10   Agree
Top Management
Disagree 1   2   3   4   5   6   7   8   9   10   Agree

14. This level of management seems to be more concerned with what is going on outside the agency than it is with what is going on inside or down in the trenches where the actual work is done. External issues and crises dominate this level of management's time.

First-Line Supervisors
Disagree 1   2   3   4   5   6   7   8   9   10   Agree
Middle Management
Disagree 1   2   3   4   5   6   7   8   9   10   Agree
Top Management
Disagree 1   2   3   4   5   6   7   8   9   10   Agree

SECTION THREE: This part of the questionnaire asks you to describe your job as objectively as you can.

Please do not use this part of the questionnaire to show how much you like or dislike your job. Questions about that will come later. Instead, try to make your description as accurate and as objective as you possibly can. A **sample** question is given below.

Sample:
Please *circle* the number that is the most accurate description of your job.
A.   To what extent does your job require you to work with mechanical equipment?

1	2	3	4	5	6	7

Very little; the
job requires almost
no contact with
mechanical equipment
of any kind.

Moderately.

Very much; the
job requires
almost constant
work with mechanical
equipment.

If, for example, your job requires you to work with mechanical equipment a good deal of the time—but also requires some paperwork—you might circle the number six.

---

1.   To what extent does your job require you to work closely with other people (either "clients," or people in related jobs in your own organization)?

1	2	3	4	5	6	7

Very little; deal-
ing with other
people is not at
all necessary in
doing the job.

Moderately;
some dealing
with others
is necessary.

Very much; dealing
with other people
is an absolutely
essential and
crucial part of
doing the job.

2.   How much autonomy is there in your job? That is, to what extent does your job permit you to decide on your own how to go about doing the work?

1	2	3	4	5	6	7

Very little; the
job gives me almost
no personal "say"
about how and when
the work is done.

Moderate autonomy;
many things are
standardized and
not under my
control, but I can
make some decisions
about the work.

Very much; the
job gives me
almost complete
responsibility
for deciding how
and when the
work is done.

3. To what extent does your job involve doing a "whole" and identifiable piece of work? That is, is the job a complete piece of work that has an obvious beginning and end? Or is it only a small part of the overall piece of work, which is finished by other people or by automated machines?

1	2	3	4	5	6	7

My job is only a tiny part of the overall piece of work; the results of my activities cannot be seen in the final product or service.

My job is a moderate-sized "chunk" of the overall piece of work; my own contribution can be seen in the final outcome.

My job involves doing the whole piece of work from start to finish; the results of my activities are easily seen in the final product or service.

4. How much variety is there in your job? That is, to what extent does the job require you to do many different things at work, using a variety of your skills and talents?

1	2	3	4	5	6	7

Very little; the job requires me to do the same routine things over and over again.

Moderate variety.

Very much; the job requires me to do many different things, using a number of different skills and talents.

5. In general, how significant or important is your job? That is, are the results of your work likely to significantly affect the lives or well-being of other people?

1	2	3	4	5	6	7

Not very significant; the outcomes of my work are not likely to have important effects on other people.

Moderately significant.

Highly significant; the outcomes of my work can affect other people in very important ways.

6. To what extent do managers or co-workers let you know how well you are doing on your job?

1	2	3	4	5	6	7

Very little; people almost never let me know how well I am doing.

Moderately; sometimes people may give me "feedback," other times they may not.

Very much; the managers or co-workers provide me with almost constant "feedback" about how well I am doing.

7. To what extent does doing the job itself provide you with information about your work performance? That is, does the actual work itself provide clues about how well you are doing—aside from any "feedback" co-workers or supervisors may provide?

1	2	3	4	5	6	7

Very little; the job itself is set up so I could work forever without finding out how well I am doing.

Moderately; sometimes doing the job provides "feedback," to me; sometimes it does not.

Very much; the job is set up so that I get almost constant "feedback" as I work about how well I am doing.

SECTION FOUR: Listed below are a number of statements that could be used to describe a job.

Please indicate whether each statement is an accurate or inaccurate description of your job.

Write a number in the blank beside each statement, based on the following scale:

1	2	3	4	5	6	7
Very Inaccurate	Mostly Inaccurate	Slightly Inaccurate	Uncertain	Slightly Accurate	Mostly Accurate	Very Accurate

_____ 1. The job requires me to use a number of complex or high-level skills.

_____ 2. The job requires a lot of cooperative work with other people.

_____ 3. The job is arranged so that I do not have the chance to do an entire piece of work from beginning to end.

_____ 4. Just doing the work required by the job provides many chances for me to figure out how well I am doing.

_____ 5. The job is quite simple and repetitive.

_____ 6. The job can be done adequately by a person working alone—without talking to or checking with other people.

_____ 7. The supervisors and co-workers on this job almost never give me any "feedback" about how well I am doing in my work.

_____ 8. This job is one where a lot of people can be affected by how well the work gets done.

_____ 9. The job denies me any chance to use my personal initiative or judgment in carrying out the work.

_____ 10. Supervisors often let me know how well they think I am performing the job.

_____ 11. The job provides me with the chance to completely finish the pieces of work I begin.

_____ 12. The job itself provides very few clues about whether I am performing well.

_____ 13. The job gives me considerable opportunity for independence and freedom in how I do the work.

_____ 14. The job itself is not very significant or important in the broader scheme of things.

SECTION FIVE: This section is divided into four subsections, each concerned with a different aspect of your job. Each part contains a number of words or phrases that could describe your job. Put a 1 in the blank before each word or phrase that does describe your job, a 2 in the blank if the word or phrase does not describe your job, or a 3 if you cannot decide.
(© Bowling Green State University, 1975)

WORK ON PRESENT JOB: Think of your present work. What is it like most of the time?

1 = Yes, does describe   2 = No, does not describe   3 = Cannot decide

____ Fascinating	____ Useful
____ Routine	____ Tiresome
____ Satisfying	____ Healthful
____ Boring	____ Challenging
____ Good	____ On your feet
____ Creative	____ Frustrating
____ Respected	____ Simple
____ Hot	____ Endless
____ Pleasant	____ Gives sense of accomplishment

OPPORTUNITIES FOR PROMOTION: Think of the opportunities for promotion that you have now. How well does each of the following words describe these?

1 = Yes, does describe   2 = No, does not describe   3 = Cannot decide

____ Good opportunities for promotion	____ Unfair promotion policy
____ Opportunity somewhat limited	____ Infrequent promotion
____ Promotion on ability	____ Regular promotion
____ Dead-end job	____ Fairly good chance for promotion
____ Good chance for promotion	

MANAGEMENT AT PRESENT JOB: Think of the kind of management you have on your job. How well does each of the following words describe this supervision?

1 = Yes, does describe   2 = No, does not describe   3 = Cannot decide

____ Asks my advice	____ Tells me where I stand
____ Hard to please	____ Annoying
____ Impolite	____ Stubborn
____ Praises good work	____ Knows job well
____ Tactful	____ Bad
____ Influential	____ Intelligent
____ Up-to-date	____ Leaves me on my own
____ Doesn't supervise enough	____ Around when needed
____ Quick tempered	____ Lazy

PEOPLE ON YOUR PRESENT JOB: Think of the majority of the people that you work with now. How well does each of the following words describe these people?

1 = Yes, does describe   2 = No, does not describe   3 = Cannot decide

____ Stimulating	____ Talk too much
____ Boring	____ Smart
____ Slow	____ Lazy
____ Ambitious	____ Unpleasant
____ Stupid	____ No privacy
____ Responsible	____ Active
____ Fast	____ Narrow interests
____ Intelligent	____ Loyal
____ Easy to make enemies	____ Hard to meet

SECTION SIX: Listed below are a number of questions designed to explore the relationship between you, the general public, and your opinions about police work. Please indicate your opinion by writing a number in the blank beside each statement, based on the following scale:

1	2	3	4	5
Strongly Agree	Agree	Undecided	Disagree	Strongly Disagree

____ 1. Most citizens are really interested in the personal and professional problems of the police.

____ 2. There are few dependable ties of any sort between police and the public.

____ 3. The public hardly ever identifies with the police.

____ 4. Friendship between the citizens and the police is easy to develop.

____ 5. I prefer to deal with my law enforcement activities rather than engage citizens in casual conversation.

____ 6. The citizens and the police work together in solving problems.

____ 7. A good police officer is one who maintains the peace by using problem-solving skills.

____ 8. A good police officer is one who maintains the peace by making arrests.

____ 9. Spokane police officers should spend more time than they do informing people about available services.

____ 10. Spokane police officers should spend more time than they do trying to understand the problems of minorities.

____ 11. Spokane police officers should spend more time than they do investigating serious crimes, serious criminals, and suspicious persons.

____ 12. Spokane police officers should spend more time talking to people about their problems.

____ 13. Spokane police officers should spend more time working with individuals and groups to solve problems.

____ 14. When you're on patrol, you always have to show that you're the boss. If you get pushed around, you lose respect.

____ 15. Without street justice, there would be no justice at all.

SECTION SEVEN: Listed below are four goals that many believe describe the police contribution to the creation of a safe and humane community.

Please rank them in terms of their importance to you, with 1 being most important and 4 being least important.

____ Increased emphasis on apprehending serious criminals
____ Empowerment of officers for problem-solving activity
____ Empowerment of citizens through partnership between the police and community
____ Increased emphasis on ticketing or arresting disorderly persons

SECTION EIGHT: The implementation of community-oriented policing programs has met with a variety of obstacles. Using the following scale, please write the number that most accurately portrays an obstacle that your department is currently facing.

1	2	3	4	5
No obstacle	Slight obstacle	Moderate obstacle	Serious obstacle	Uncertain

____ 1. Resistance from middle management
____ 2. Community concern that community-oriented policing is "soft" on crime
____ 3. Police officers concerned that community-oriented policing is "soft" on crime
____ 4. Police union resistance
____ 5. Problems in line-level accountability
____ 6. Departmental confusion over what community-oriented policing is
____ 7. Lack of support from city government
____ 8. Lack of focused community-oriented police training
____ 9. Problems in balancing increased COP activities with other activities
____ 10. Other—please list _____

SECTION NINE: This section is directed principally toward patrol officers. It asks about specific problems that you may encounter in the area where you work. Using the following scale, please write the number that most accurately describes the extent of these problems in your own work. NOTE: If this section does not relate to your work, go on to Section Ten.

1	2	3	4
No problem	A problem	Serious problem	Uncertain

____ 1. Drunk drivers
____ 2. Groups of teenagers or others hanging out and harassing people
____ 3. Vandalism—that is, kids or others breaking windows, writing things on walls, or damaging property
____ 4. Garbage/litter on streets and sidewalks
____ 5. Inadequate city government services
____ 6. Physical decay—such as abandoned cars, run-down buildings, houses in disrepair, etc.
____ 7. Victimization of elderly

____ 8. People drinking in public
____ 9. Lack of community interest in crime prevention activities
____ 10. Violent crime—assaults, robberies, etc.
____ 11. Property crime—burglary, stealing things   Patrol Officers
____ 12. Juvenile crime   Indicate your sector
____ 13. Drugs   ____ Adam
____ 14. Traffic problems (congestion, speeding, etc.)   ____ Baker
____ 15. Prostitution   ____ Charlie
____ 16. Police-community relations   ____ David
____ 17. Youth gangs
____ 18. Noise
____ 19. Child abuse/neglect
____ 20. Other—Please list_____

SECTION TEN: This section asks about specific problems you may encounter in your work. Using the following scale, please write the number that most accurately describes the extent of these problems in your work.

1	2	3	4
No problem	A problem	Serious problem	Uncertain

____ 1. Excessive workload
____ 2. Inadequate equipment/technology
____ 3. Inadequate staff
____ 4. Inadequately specific policies/procedures
____ 5. Inadequate supervision/direction
____ 6. Poor working conditions (space, lighting, furniture, etc.)
____ 7. Inadequate budget resources
____ 8. "Too much red tape"
____ 9. Other. Please specify: _____

SECTION ELEVEN: This section pertains to your personal values. The task here is to arrange 18 values in order of their importance to YOU, as guiding principles in YOUR life. Study the list carefully and pick out the one value that is the most important to you. Then pick out the one value that is the second most important for you, and continue in this manner until you list the value that is least important for you in box 18. Please take your time and change your ranking as often as you wish.

1. _____   A COMFORTABLE LIFE
        (a prosperous life)

2. _____   AN EXCITING LIFE
        (a stimulating, active life)

3. _____   A SENSE OF ACCOMPLISHMENT
        (making lasting contribution)

4. _____   A WORLD AT PEACE
        (free of war and conflict)

5. _____ A WORLD OF BEAUTY
      (honor nature and the arts)

6. _____ EQUALITY
      (brotherhood and equal opportunity for all)

7. _____ FAMILY SECURITY
      (taking care of loved ones)

8. _____ FREEDOM
      (independence, free choice)

9. _____ HAPPINESS
      (contentedness)

10. _____ INNER HARMONY
      (free from internal conflict)

11. _____ MATURE LOVE
      (sexual & spiritual intimacy)

12. _____ NATIONAL SECURITY
      (protection from attack)

13. _____ PLEASURE
      (an enjoyable, leisurely life)

14._____ SALVATION
      (saved, achieve eternal life)

15._____ SELF-RESPECT
      (self-esteem)

16._____ SOCIAL RECOGNITION
      (respect and admiration of others)

17._____ TRUE FRIENDSHIP
      (close companionship)

18._____ WISDOM
      (a mature understanding of life)

Finally, did you complete the 1993 Employee Survey conducted by Washington State University?

_____ Yes   _____ No   _____ Unsure

COMMENTS ON THE EMPLOYEE SURVEY

Please record any comments brought to mind by filling out this survey.

Appendix B

Focus Group Questions for SPD Internal Groups

As a Spokane police officer, what is your impression of the community in general?

What is your impression of community-oriented policing philosophy?

Would you say that your role as a police officer is more crime control (that is, enforcement oriented) or order maintenance (for example, problem solving)?

Under the COP philosophy, you are expected to act as a problem solver. What expectations do you have of the department to aid you in this problem-solving role?

What level of support have you received from the department when engaged in problem-solving activities? From supervisors? Lieutenants (mid-management)? Captains (management)? Chiefs (top management)? Peers?

How much time would you say you spend "on the beat" as opposed to filling out paperwork?

Aside from your usual law enforcement duties, how much of your typical day is spent solving community problems?

What sort of input would you say you have into the functioning of the Spokane Police Department? (In other words, if you had any suggestions as to how police operations could be more effective, do you feel that your thoughts would be given consideration?)

Do Spokane police officers treat all citizens equally?

Do you believe the job you do contributes to the quality of life in Spokane?

What types of training do you see as essential for police in order to entertain a community policing philosophy throughout the department?

In what ways can performance evaluations be modified to reflect a better profile of officer performance?

How often should performance evaluations be conducted?

Appendix C

Pullman Police Department
Crime and Criminal Justice Survey
1995

In the interest of assessing its services to the public, the Pullman Police Department has asked the Washington State Institute for Community-Oriented Policing at Washington State University-Spokane to administer a survey to a representative sample of Pullman residents. You have been selected at random as one of 800 people who can help define public opinion in this very important study.

The results of this study will be used by the Pullman Police Department to identify specific ways to better serve its citizens. We are asking for about 15 to 20 minutes of your time to complete the survey and return it to Washington State University in the postage pre-paid envelope provided.

Your participation is **VOLUNTARY** and your answers are entirely **CONFIDENTIAL**. Only the researchers at Washington State University-Spokane will see your answers and comments. The Pullman Police Department will receive only a report of the general findings in grouped form.

Thank you for your assistance in this effort to determine how the citizens of Pullman view the efforts of the Pullman Police Department.

Sincerely,

William T. Weatherly, Jr.
Chief of Police
ID#

NOTE: The ID number on this questionnaire is used only to coordinate mailings. When you return your survey, your number is checked off our mailing list and you will not be bothered by follow-up contacts.

SECTION ONE: This section asks your opinion of the services provided by Pullman police officers in terms of the **LEVEL** and **QUALITY** of services provided.

The following questions relate to the level and quality of service provided by the Pullman Police Department.

Please answer the following questions keeping in mind the following definitions:

LEVEL of service: the amount or frequency of the provision of services. For example, how frequently do police officers patrol your neighborhood or offer service?

QUALITY of service: how good are the services that are provided? For example, how courteous, professional, and effective are police officers in their contacts with the public?

1.   Please indicate your opinion of the **LEVEL** of service provided by the Pullman Police Department. (Please check one.)

    ___NOT AN ADEQUATE LEVEL OF SERVICE   ___TOO HIGH A LEVEL OF SERVICE

    ___ABOUT THE RIGHT LEVEL OF SERVICE   ___DO NOT KNOW ENOUGH TO JUDGE

2.   Please indicate your opinion about the **QUALITY** of service provided by the Pullman Police Department. (Please check one.)

    ___ POOR   ___ FAIR   ___ GOOD   ___ EXCELLENT   ___ DON'T KNOW

3.   Overall, the Pullman Police Department does a good job at providing both the **QUALITY** and **LEVEL OF SERVICE** in your community. (Please check one.)

    ___ STRONGLY AGREE   ___ AGREE   ___ UNDECIDED   ___ DISAGREE
    ___ STRONGLY DISAGREE

4.   Thinking about the number of police you see in your neighborhood, would you say that there are TOO MANY, TOO FEW, or ABOUT THE RIGHT NUMBER? (Please check one.)

    ___ TOO MANY   ___ TOO FEW
    ___ ABOUT THE RIGHT NUMBER   ___ DON'T KNOW/NO OPINION

5.   Do you know any of the police officers working in your neighborhood? That is, have you seen a particular officer around here enough times that you would be able to recognize him or her if you saw them again? (Please check one.)

    ___ YES   ___ NO

SECTION TWO: Questions in this section ask about specific problems that may exist in your neighborhood. Using the following scale, please write the number that most accurately describes the extent of these problems.

(1) NO PROBLEM   (2) A PROBLEM   (3) SERIOUS PROBLEM   (4) UNCERTAIN

____ People's homes being broken into and things stolen
____ People being robbed or having their purses/wallets taken
____ People breaking into cars
____ Auto theft
____ People being beaten up
____ Rape
____ Domestic violence
____ Drunk drivers
____ Groups of teenagers or others hanging out and harassing people
____ Youth gangs
____ People using and/or dealing in illegal drugs
____ Child abuse/neglect
____ Vandalism—that is, kids or others breaking windows, writing things on walls,
        damaging mailboxes or other property
____ Inadequate patrol services
____ Inadequate city government services
____ Physical decay—such as abandoned cars, run-down buildings, houses in disrepair, etc.
____ Victimization of the elderly
____ Lack of community interest in crime prevention activities
____ Police-community relations
____ Garbage/litter on streets and sidewalks
____ Parking problems
____ Bicycle violations/safety
____ Stray animals
____ Traffic problems (congestion, speeding, etc.)
____ Noise—such as barking dogs, loud parties, and juvenile drinking
____ Other (Please specify.)

1. Now, go back to the above list and circle the most serious problem in your neighborhood. Next, please rate how much of an **EFFORT** Pullman police officers make in responding to and resolving the **MOST SERIOUS** problem you identified from the list above. (Please check one.)

    ___ EXCELLENT ___ VERY GOOD ___ GOOD ___ FAIR ___ POOR ___NOT SURE

2. Does the elementary school in your neighborhood have a DARE program? (Please check one.)

    ___ YES   ___ NO   ___ DON'T KNOW

3. Have you or your child(ren) ever been involved with a DARE program?

    ___ YES   ___ NO

4.   How EFFECTIVE do you feel the DARE program in Pullman is in educating children about the dangers of drug abuse? (Please circle one.)

    1   2   3   4   5   6   7   8
NOT EFFECTIVE   VERY EFFECTIVE   DON'T KNOW

SECTION THREE: Listed below are 20 items designed to explore the relationship between the general public and the Pullman Police Department. Please indicate YOUR opinion by writing a number in the blank beside each statement, based on the following scale:

1—STRONGLY AGREE
2—AGREE
3—UNDECIDED
4—DISAGREE
5—STRONGLY DISAGREE

____ Most citizens are really interested in the problems faced by Pullman police officers.
____ There are few dependable personal ties between patrol officers and the public.
____ Friendship between the citizens and the patrol officers is easy to develop.
____ Patrol officers seem content staying in their patrol cars rather than interacting with the citizens.
____ The citizens and Pullman police officers work together in solving problems.
____ Pullman police officers are usually fair.
____ Pullman police officers are usually courteous.
____ Pullman police officers are usually honest.
____ Pullman police officers are usually intimidating.
____ In general, Pullman police officers treat all citizens equally according to the law.
____ Pullman police officers show concern when asked questions.
____ Only the police department can control crime in Pullman.
____ Pullman police officers are more strict in some neighborhoods than in others.
____ A good police officer is one who maintains the peace by using creativity to solve problems relating to public safety.
____ A good police officer is one who maintains the peace by making frequent arrests.
____ Pullman police officers should spend more time than they do informing people about available services.
____ Pullman police officers should spend more time talking to people about their problems.
____ Pullman police officers should spend more time than they do investigating serious crimes, serious criminals, and suspicious persons.
____ Pullman police officers should spend more time working with individuals and groups to solve problems.
____ I believe patrol officers must patrol for relatively minor law violations if there is to be general compliance with laws in our community.
____ Pullman police officers should spend more time on traffic enforcement.

SECTION FOUR: In this section we would like to learn about your neighborhood. By the term neighborhood, we mean the area within a 15-minute walk of your home. (Please indicate your response to each item with a check mark.)

1. Were you raised in the same neighborhood (within a 15-minute walk) as you now live?
    ___ YES   ___ NO

2. Would you describe your neighborhood as a place where people help one another or where people go their own way?
    _____ PEOPLE HELP ONE ANOTHER   _____ PEOPLE GO THEIR OWN WAY

3. Do you feel your neighborhood is more of a "real home" or more like "just a place to live?"
    _____ REAL HOME   _____ JUST A PLACE TO LIVE

4. How **safe do you feel** walking alone during the day in your neighborhood?
    ____ VERY SAFE   ____ SAFE   ____ NEITHER SAFE NOR UNSAFE
    ____ UNSAFE   ____ VERY UNSAFE

5. How **safe do you feel** being outside and alone in your neighborhood at night?
    ____ VERY SAFE   ____ SAFE   ____ NEITHER SAFE NOR UNSAFE
    ____ UNSAFE   ____ VERY UNSAFE

6. How likely is it for local groups or organizations to get government officials to respond to a neighborhood problem?
    _____ VERY LIKELY _____ SOMEWHAT LIKELY
    _____ SOMEWHAT UNLIKELY   _____VERY UNLIKELY

7. Overall, how satisfied are you with your neighborhood?
    _____ VERY SATISFIED   _____ SATISFIED _____ SOMEWHAT SATISFIED
    _____ DISSATISFIED _____ VERY DISSATISFIED

8. If a neighbor of yours was having trouble with rowdy teenagers parking in front of their residence, which of the following would you be most likely to do?
    _____ NOT GET INVOLVED   _____ CALL THE POLICE DEPARTMENT
    _____ GET WITH THE NEIGHBOR TO ADDRESS THE PROBLEM

9. How often do you walk/jog or ride a bicycle in your neighborhood?
    _____OFTEN _____ SOMETIMES _____ RARELY _____ NEVER

10. How often do you worry about your own personal safety in your neighborhood?
    _____OFTEN _____ SOMETIMES _____ RARELY _____ NEVER

11. How often do you worry about your children's safety in your neighborhood?
    _____OFTEN _____ SOMETIMES _____ RARELY _____ NEVER

12. How often do you shop in Pullman?
    _____OFTEN _____ SOMETIMES _____ RARELY _____ NEVER

13. How willing are you to help the police department improve the quality of life in your neighborhood—for example, go to meetings or make phone calls to neighbors?
    _____ VERY WILLING   _____ WILLING
    _____ NEITHER WILLING NOR UNWILLING
    _____ UNWILLING   _____ VERY UNWILLING

Please respond to the following two statements:

14. The local government is concerned about your neighborhood.
    ____ STRONGLY AGREE   ____ AGREE
    ____ NEITHER AGREE NOR DISAGREE
    ____ DISAGREE   ____ STRONGLY DISAGREE

15. It is difficult to gain any satisfaction from talking to the public officials in your community.
    ____ STRONGLY AGREE   ____ AGREE
    ____ NEITHER AGREE NOR DISAGREE
    ____ DISAGREE   ____ STRONGLY DISAGREE

SECTION FIVE: This section asks whether you are familiar with programs run by the Pullman Police Department. Please indicate whether you are familiar with any of the following programs:

	YES, I AM FAMILIAR WITH	NO, I AM NOT FAMILIAR WITH
1. DARE	_____	_____
2. School Resource Officers	_____	_____
3. Block (Crime) Watch	_____	_____
4. Bicycle Patrol	_____	_____
5. Neighborhood Resource Officer	_____	_____
6. Citizens Academy	_____	_____
7. Police Department Open House	_____	_____

Have you participated in any of these programs? _____ YES   _____ NO

If yes, please list:

_____

Given the limitations on budget and staffing, how much priority should the Pullman Police Department give to the following: (Please check the one that is most important.)

_____ DARE
_____ TRAFFIC ENFORCEMENT
_____ DWI
_____ BLOCK WATCH/ENFORCEMENT PATROL CRIME PREVENTION
_____ DRUGS/DRUG DEALERS
_____ DOWNTOWN FOOT PATROL
_____ RANDOM NEIGHBORHOOD CRIME PREVENTION

SECTION SIX: In this section, you will be asked questions about local programs and policies and your support for them.

The Pullman Police Department is guided by the philosophy of Community Oriented Policing. Some of the programs that have evolved from Community Policing are DARE, foot patrol, and programs aimed at crime prevention.

Please indicate whether you AGREE or DISAGREE with the following statements concerning police priorities and COP programs.

1. I think police should concentrate more on catching criminals than on working with the public.
    ____ STRONGLY AGREE   ____ AGREE   ____ UNDECIDED
    ____ DISAGREE   ____ STRONGLY DISAGREE

2. I think this is a good use of police resources if it can be shown that these programs lead to reduced crime.
    ____ STRONGLY AGREE   ____ AGREE   ____ UNDECIDED
    ____ DISAGREE   ____ STRONGLY DISAGREE

3. I think police should put more officers on the streets even if that means reducing other services such as traffic control, crime analysis, volunteer services, and other non-patrol functions.
    ____ STRONGLY AGREE   ____ AGREE   ____ UNDECIDED
    ____ DISAGREE   ____ STRONGLY DISAGREE

4. I think Community Oriented Policing is just another name for coddling criminals and people on welfare.
    ____ STRONGLY AGREE   ____ AGREE   ____ UNDECIDED
    ____ DISAGREE   ____ STRONGLY DISAGREE'

5. I think Community Oriented Policing sounds like the direction all police will have to take if we are to reduce drugs, gangs, and crime.
    ____ STRONGLY AGREE   ____ AGREE   ____ UNDECIDED
    ____ DISAGREE   ____ STRONGLY DISAGREE

6. I think the City Council should hire more police officers even if other essential city services have to be cut.
    ____ STRONGLY AGREE   ____ AGREE   ____ UNDECIDED
    ____ DISAGREE   ____ STRONGLY DISAGREE

7. I think citizens must take more responsibility through programs such as Block Watch for the safety of their neighborhoods. More police officers alone can never solve the problems of crime.
    ____ STRONGLY AGREE   ____ AGREE   ____ UNDECIDED
    ____ DISAGREE   ____ STRONGLY DISAGREE

SECTION SEVEN: In this section you will be asked questions about your contacts with Pullman police officers, your previous victimizations (if any), and your perceptions of safety in your neighborhood.

1.   In the past 6 months how many personal contacts have you had with the Pullman Police Department? (Please check one.)

     ____ NONE   ____ ONE   ____ TWO   ____ THREE OR MORE

2.   The reason for your MOST RECENT contact in the past six months was: (Please check one.)
     ____ Traffic violation
     ____ Information/request for service
     ____ Visited jail
     ____ Incarcerated in jail
     ____ Arrested
     ____ Reported crime
     ____ Had no contact
     ____ Other _____

3.   The quality of this MOST RECENT contact was: (Please check one.)
     ____ POOR   ____ FAIR   ____ GOOD   ____ EXCELLENT   ____ HAD NO CONTACT

4.   Receiving a traffic citation (ticket) is never a pleasant experience. If you have ever received a traffic ticket from a Pullman police officer, did you feel you were treated fairly?
     YES_____   NO_____   NOT APPLICABLE (No citation.)_____

5.   In the past 6 months, have you been a victim of any of the following crimes? (Please check ALL that apply.)
     ____ No, I have not been a victim in the last 6 months.
     (IF NO, PLEASE SKIP QUESTIONS 6 AND 7.)
     ____ **Assault** (an unlawful attack by one person upon another for the purpose of inflicting bodily injury)
     ____ **Robbery** (the taking or attempting to take anything of value from the care, custody, or control of a person by force or threat of force and/or by putting the victim in fear)
     ____ **Burglary** (the unlawful entry of a structure to commit a felony or a theft)
     ____ **Larceny-theft** (the unlawful taking, carrying, leading, or riding away of property from the possession of another)
     ____ **Racial/Sexual harassment** (victim of racial or sexual "hate crime")
     ____ **Automobile theft** (the theft or attempted theft of a motor vehicle)
     ____ **Vandalism** (willful or malicious destruction, injury, disfigurement, or defacement of any public or private property without the consent of the owner)
     ____ Other (Please specify.) _____

6.   Did you report your last criminal victimization to the Pullman Police Department?
     ____ YES   ____ NO (If NO, please skip question 7.)

7. Please indicate your level of satisfaction with the Pullman Police Department's response to your most recent victimization.

	1	2	3	4	5	6	7
	VERY SATISFIED						DISSATISFIED

8. If you have ever used the Self-Reporting Property Crime Report provided by the Pullman Police Department, please indicate your level of satisfaction with this procedure.

	1	2	3	4	5	6	7
	VERY SATISFIED						DISSATISFIED

SECTION EIGHT: These questions ask about your background. This information is needed in order to ensure that people from all walks of life are represented in the survey.

1. Please indicate the year of your birth: 19___.

2. Ethnic background (Please check one.)
    ____ ASIAN-AMERICAN   ____ NATIVE AMERICAN/INDIAN
    ____ BLACK/AFRICAN-AMERICAN   ____ LATINO
    ____ CAUCASIAN/WHITE   ____ OTHER (Please specify.)
    ____ MEXICAN-AMERICAN/HISPANIC
                                   _____

3. Gender (Please check one.)
    ____ MALE   ____ FEMALE

4. Please check the highest level of schooling you have completed:
    ____ NOT A HIGH SCHOOL GRADUATE   ____ HIGH SCHOOL GRADUATE
    ____ SOME COLLEGE   ____ ASSOCIATE DEGREE
    (*degree not completed*)
    ____ BACHELOR'S DEGREE   ____ SOME GRADUATE COURSEWORK
                                       (*degree not completed*)
    ____ GRADUATE DEGREE   ____ OTHER (Please specify.)

5. What is your present **occupation**? (If retired, please put an "X" in this blank ____, and mark your former occupation.)

SELF-EMPLOYED	EMPLOYED	OTHER
____ Construction, fisherman, etc.	____ Manual worker (blue	____ Homemaker
____ Professional (lawyer,	collar, etc.)	____ Student
accountant, doctor, etc.)	____ White collar (office	____ Unemployed
	worker, staff, etc.)	
	____ Executive (management, director, etc.)	
____ Business owner	____ Other: _____	

6. What is the total number of persons in your household?_____

7. Please record the number of school-age children currently living in your household. _____

8. What is the size of your family? _____ # OF ADULTS _____ # OF CHILDREN

9. Please indicate your approximate family income before taxes in 1993.
    ____ less than $6,999   ____ $25,000-$29,999
    ____ $7,000-$9,999   ____ $30,000-$49,999
    ____ $10,000-$14,999   ____ $50,000-$74,999
    ____ $15,000-$19,999   ____ $75,000 and over
    ____ $20,000-$24,999

10. Are you a homeowner or a renter?
    ____ HOMEOWNER   ____ RENTER

11. Type of residence (Please check one.)
    ____ APARTMENT   ____ MOBILE HOME
    ____ SINGLE FAMILY HOME ____ CONDOMINIUM
    ____ DUPLEX   ____ OTHER

12. In what area of the city do you live?
    ____ NORTH ____ SOUTH ____ EAST ____ WEST

13. What is the name of the neighborhood (e.g., Military Hill, College Hill, etc.) in which you live? _____

14. How would you describe the area of the city in which you live?
    ____ MOSTLY URBAN ____ SMALL TOWN ____ MOSTLY RURAL

15. How long have you lived in Pullman? ____ YEARS

16. Were you born in Pullman?
    ____ YES ____ NO

17. Where would you place yourself on the following scale regarding political outlook? (Please check the appropriate space.)

    VERY   MIDDLE OF
    LIBERAL _____   LIBERAL _____ THE ROAD _____   CONSERVATIVE _____

    VERY CONSERVATIVE _____

18. Compared to the average citizen, how well-informed would you say you are on crime and criminal justice issues?

    LESS   EQUALLY WELL-   BETTER
    INFORMED ____   INFORMED ____   INFORMED ____

19. In general, patrol services in Pullman have been:

GETTING WORSE   GETTING BETTER
THE PAST COUPLE   1   2   3   4   5   6   7   THE PAST
OF YEARS   COUPLE OF YEARS

                                    STAYING
                                    THE SAME

20. In general, crime in Pullman has been:

GETTING WORSE   GETTING BETTER
THE PAST COUPLE   1   2   3   4   5   6   7   THE PAST
OF YEARS   COUPLE OF YEARS

                                    STAYING
                                    THE SAME

21. How do you rate Pullman as a place to live?
_____ EXCELLENT   _____ VERY GOOD   _____ FAIR   _____ POOR

22. Do you consider Pullman a safe place to live?
_____ YES   _____ NO

COMMENTS: We would appreciate any observations or suggestions you would like to record. Your comments will receive our careful attention.

THANK YOU FOR YOUR COOPERATION IN THIS IMPORTANT UNDERTAKING!

Appendix D

Proposed Focus Group Questions for Pasco PD Project

What are your perceptions of the police in general (that is, all police—not just Pasco police officers)?

How do your perceptions concerning the Pasco police compare with your perceptions of police in general? (Are there any similarities or differences?)

Have you interacted with the Pasco Police Department? (If so, in what capacity?)

What was your overall impression of your interaction with the Pasco police?

Would you say that the Pasco police are usually fair and courteous?

Would you say that the Pasco police treat all citizens equally under the law?

Would you say that Pasco police must patrol for minor law violations (for example, vandalism, rowdy teens, public drunkenness) if there is to be general compliance with the laws in your community?

Do you feel safe walking alone in your neighborhood during the day? How about at night?

Do you worry about your own personal safety in your neighborhood?

How willing are you to help the Pasco Police Department improve the quality of life in your neighborhood?

How can the Pasco Police Department make your community a safer place to live?

What specific traits do you feel are essential for today's police officers?

Do you believe that the Pasco Police Department has a reputation, and if so, for what?

Author Index

Subject Index

About the Authors

Socorro Benitez is an Assistant Professor of Criminal Justice at Eastern Washington University. Professor Benitez is in the process of completing her doctorate in Political Science at Washington State University, where she previously served as a research associate with the Washington Institute for Community-Oriented Policing.

Michael L. Birzer is Assistant Professor of Criminal Justice at Washburn University in Topeka, Kansas. He received both bachelor's and master's degrees in administration of justice at Wichita State University and earned his doctorate from Oklahoma State University. Prior to becoming an assistant professor in 1999, Dr. Birzer spent 18 years with the Sedgwick County Sheriff's Department in Wichita, where he attained the rank of lieutenant. His research interests include police training and learning strategies, community policing, and the dynamics of organizational change.

Michael W. Brand is an assistant professor at the University of Oklahoma. He received his Ph.D. in Social Work from the University of Texas-Arlington. In addition to teaching, consultation, and clinical practice, he is involved in community practice and research, which includes community policing in rural communities.

Gary Cordner is Dean of the College of Justice and Safety (formerly the College of Law Enforcement) at Eastern Kentucky University, where he is also a Professor of Police Studies and Director of the Regional Community Policing Institute. He received his doctorate from Michigan State University and served as a police officer and police chief in Maryland. Dr. Cordner has coauthored textbooks on police administration and criminal justice planning and coedited the volumes *What Works in Policing?*; *Police Operations: Analysis and Evaluation*; *Managing Police Organizations*; *Managing Police Personnel;* and *Policing Perspectives: An Anthology*. He edited the *American Journal of Police* from 1987 to 1992, coedited *Police Computer Review* from 1992 to 1995, and now edits *Police Quarterly*. Dr. Cordner is past-president of the Academy of Criminal Justice Sciences, the country's largest association of criminal justice educators and researchers, as well as a founder and former chair of that organization's Police Section.

John P. Crank received his Ph.D. from the University of Colorado and currently is Professor of Criminal Justice Administration at Boise State University. Dr. Crank continues to study police organizations and police subculture and has published dozens of articles on these and related subjects. He is author of *Understanding Police Culture* and coauthor (with Michael Caldero) of *Police Ethics: The Corruption of Noble Cause.*

David E. Duffee is Professor of the School of Criminal Justice, State University of New York at Albany. From 1988-1995 he served as Dean of the School. Dr. Duffee is the principal investigator for the Police-Community Interaction Project (PCIP) in the National Institute of Justice's "Measuring What Matters" program. PCIP is developing measures of the ways in which police and neighborhood groups interact. Dr. Duffee is editor of *Measurement* *and Analysis of Crime and Justice*, volume 4, in the National Institute of Justice series *Criminal Justice 2000*. He also (with Edward Maguire) is coediting a volume, *Criminal Justice Theory* for Wadsworth.

James Frank is an associate professor in the Division of Criminal Justice at the University of Cincinnati. During the last four years he has directed two police observation studies that examined the work routines of street-level officers employed by the Cincinnati Police Division and 21 small-town and rural police agencies. His primary research interests are in the areas of officer decision making, police use of technology, and the evaluation of police policies. He has published policing articles in *Justice Quarterly;* the *American Journal of Police; Journal of Criminal Justice;* and *Policing: International Journal of Police Strategies and Management.*

Andrew L. Giacomazzi is Assistant Professor of Criminal Justice Administration at Boise State University. Dr. Giacomazzi received his Ph.D. in political science at Washington State University in 1995. He is a coauthor (with Quint Thurman and Jihong Zhao) of *Community Policing in a Community Era: An Introduction and Exploration.* His most recent articles have appeared in *Justice Research and Policy; Crime and Delinquency; Police Studies;* and *Justice Quarterly.* His research interests include community policing, organizational change, and family violence. Dr. Giacomazzi is principal investigator of an evaluation to determine the effects of organizational and community assessments on change toward community policing in five western states.

Ricky S. Gutierrez is an assistant professor in the Division of Criminal Justice at California State University-Sacramento. His research interests include policing, organizational change, juvenile justice, policy impact analysis, and criminal justice system technology issues. Since the publication of the first edition of *Community Policing in a Rural Setting*, Professor Gutierrez has been involved in gathering data from more than 450 law enforcement agencies that have received federal funding from the Office of Community Oriented Policing Services (OCOPS).

Carl W. Hawkins, Jr. is a Major with the Hillsborough County Sheriff's Office in Tampa, Florida. He has 27 years of law enforcement experience and has worked in every administrative and operational department at the sheriff's office. Dr. Hawkins has a D.P.A. degree (1982) from Nova Southeastern University and completed a community policing fellowship at the Federal Law Enforcement Training Center in Glynco, Georgia. His most recent publication (with Tom Payne) appears in *Controversial Issues in Policing* (1999). Dr. Hawkins teaches in the Criminology Program at the University of South Florida, the Command Officers Program of the Southern Police Institute at the University of Louisville, and the Law Enforcement Executive Program at North Carolina State University.

Cary Heck received his Ph.D. in Political Science from Washington State University in 1998. He currently serves as the Assistant Director of Training of the Juvenile Corrections Program with Louisiana State University's Health Sciences Center in New Orleans. Dr. Heck administers a program that prepares and delivers training to Louisiana juvenile corrections staff and administrators concerning issues of juvenile delinquency and medical and mental health issues within juvenile correctional facilities. He previously worked for the U.S. Department of Justice and at both Arizona State and Boise State Universities. Dr. Heck's other publications include topics ranging from issues in policing to the causes of delinquency.

Steven T. Kernes has served as Chief, State and Local Programs Division, National Center for State and Local Law Enforcement Training since 1990. Previously, he was sheriff of Clallam County, Washington, and Director of Emergency Services from 1979 to 1990. He managed a full-service law enforcement agency, 120-bed jail, and was responsible for emergency management. From 1965 through 1979, he served in various capacities and assignments with the National Park Service, which included five years as a criminal investigator for the Olympic National Park, Washington.

John Liederbach is Assistant Professor of Criminal Justice at the University of North Texas. He completed his doctoral studies in Criminal Justice at the University of Cincinnati and recently served as the site director of a National Institute of Justice study that examined the behavior of officers employed by small-town and rural police agencies. His research interests also include the study of police officer behavior and research on white-collar crime.

Edmund F. McGarrell is Professor and Director of the School of Criminal Justice at Michigan State University. He previously taught in the Department of Criminal Justice at Indiana University, where he also directed the Crime Control Policy Center at the Indianapolis-based Hudson Institute. He has been a fellow at the National Center for Juvenile Justice and was formerly the codirector of the Washington State Institute for Community Oriented Policing. His current research includes strategic problem solving to reduce violent crime through the Department of Justice's Strategic Approaches to Community Safety Initiative, former inmate reentry, and the use of restorative justice conferences for juvenile offenders. Dr. McGarrell's research has been supported by the National Institute of Justice, the Office of Juvenile Justice and Delinquency Prevention, and a number of private foundations.

David G. Mueller is an assistant professor in the Department of Criminal Justice Administration at Boise State University. He received his B.A. from San Jose State University and his M.A. and Ph.D. from Washington State University in Pullman. Dr. Mueller's research interests include community- and school-based juvenile delinquency prevention, program evaluation, and community policing. His most recent research project examines the utility of TEAM as a police-initiated school-based prevention program and alternative to DARE.

Kathryn E. Scarborough is an associate professor in the College of Justice and Safety, Department of Criminal Justice and Police Studies, at Eastern Kentucky University, where she is also Director of Research and Evaluation in the Justice and Safety Center and Co-Director of the Regional Community Policing Institute. She is a former police officer and United States Navy veteran. She received a bachelor's degree in Criminal Justice from the University of Southern Mississippi, a master's degree in Applied Sociology from Old Dominion and Norfolk State Universities, with a certificate in Women's Studies, and a Ph.D. in Criminal Justice from Sam Houston State University. Her research and teaching interests include women in law enforcement, community policing, police administration, law enforcement technology, and violence against women.

Quint C. Thurman is Professor and Chair of the Department of Criminal Justice at Southwest Texas State University in San Marcos, Texas. Dr. Thurman earned the Ph.D. in Sociology from the University at Massachusetts (Amherst) in 1987. He since has directed criminal justice programs in Washington and Kansas prior to joining the Criminal Justice faculty at Southwest Texas State in 2001. A native Oklahoman, Dr. Thurman's B.A. and M.A. degrees are from the University of Oklahoma. He has published three books and dozens of articles, which have appeared in journals such as the *American Behavioral Scientist; Crime and Delinquency; Social Science Quarterly; American Journal of Police; Policing; Justice Quarterly*; and the *Journal of Quantitative Criminology*. He most recently published *Community Policing in a Community Era* with coauthors Jihong Zhao and Andrew Giacomazzi.

Ralph Weisheit is Distinguished Professor of Criminal Justice at Illinois State University. He has published six books, more than 30 articles in professional journals, and has contributed more than 10 chapters to edited books. His current research interests include rural crime, rural justice systems, and illicit drugs. Dr. Weisheit has appeared on the news program *60 Minutes* and on the PBS documentary series *Frontline*, as well as the CNBC program *America's Talking*. His work has also been reported in *The Atlantic Monthly, U.S. News and World Report*, and has been featured in *U.S.A. Today*.

Jihong "Solomon" Zhao is Associate Professor of Criminal Justice at the University of Nebraska-Omaha. Dr. Zhao received his Ph.D. in political science at Washington State University in 1994. He is the author of *Why Police Organizations Change: A Study of Community Oriented Policing* and coauthor (with Quint Thurman and Andrew Giacomazzi) of *Community Policing in a Community Era: An Introduction and Exploration*. His most recent articles have appeared in *Crime and Delinquency; Journal of Criminal Justice*; and *Justice Quarterly*. His research interests include evaluating police innovations and organizational change, especially as these issues pertain to community policing. Dr. Zhao currently is working with the Office of Community Oriented Policing Services to assess the relationship between federal funding for community policing and crime reduction.

Made in the USA
Columbia, SC
06 June 2019